Mary Elizabeth Blake

A Summer Holiday in Europe

Mary Elizabeth Blake

A Summer Holiday in Europe

ISBN/EAN: 9783337289461

Printed in Europe, USA, Canada, Australia, Japan

Cover: Foto ©Andreas Hilbeck / pixelio.de

More available books at **www.hansebooks.com**

A SUMMER HOLIDAY
IN EUROPE

BY

MARY ELIZABETH BLAKE
AUTHOR OF "MEXICO — PICTURESQUE, POLITICAL, PROGRESSIVE" "POEMS"
"ON THE WING" ETC.

BOSTON MDCCCXCI
LEE AND SHEPARD PUBLISHERS
10 MILK STREET NEXT "THE OLD SOUTH MEETING HOUSE"
NEW YORK CHARLES T. DILLINGHAM
718 AND 720 BROADWAY

CONTENTS.

INTRODUCTION ix

CHAPTER I.
THE VOYAGE—
The ship: sitting on deck—An epitome of life—The heart of the ship—Sailing along the Irish coast—Queenstown and harbour—The spring growth, and the young birds—Cork . . . 1-10

CHAPTER II.
GLENGARIFF AND KILLARNEY—
Presence of soldiers—Police—Government by force—Restrictions of property—Stamp of royalty—Roadside pictures—Showers—Glengariff—Hotel—The drive to Killarney . . . 13-22

CHAPTER III.
DUBLIN AND SUBURBS—
Character of warmth in the people—Courtesy of the shopkeepers—Rambles—Historic places—Trinity College—Killiney—Bray—The Hospitals—The country 23-30

CHAPTER IV.
FIRST IMPRESSIONS OF PARIS—
The journey to Paris—Impressions from the district and scenery—Women at work—The dazzle and brightness of Paris—The great square of the Place de la Concord—Historic contrasts and effects—Provisions in markets, shops, cafés . . . 33-40

CHAPTER V.
A FESTIVAL DAY IN PARIS—
Opening of the Exposition—All the nationalities in gala dress—The Trocadero—The Exposition—The welcome of the President—The opening: the night illuminations—Crowds . . 41-48

CHAPTER VI.

THE GREAT EXPOSITION—

Beauty and arrangement of the grounds—The Eiffel Tower—The joy of the people—The triumph of industry—The Pavilion of Liberal Arts—Painting and sculpture—Fine arts . . . 49-56

CHAPTER VII.

THE VICTORIES OF PEACE AND LABOUR—

The Exposition—A world's fair—The International Congresses—Questions of philanthropy, industry, inventions, temperance, peace, &c.—Artistic influences—Paris a city of leisure . . 57-64

CHAPTER VIII.

AMONG THE PARIS CHURCHES—

Notre Dame—The Madeleine—Funerals—The poorer classes—The struggles of the Communists—New Paris—Old Paris . 65-72

CHAPTER IX.

THE PARISIAN AT HOME—

Attractions of the city to the people—Cheap enjoyments—The comforts—The cleanings—Habits of life, meals—Temperance of the people—Entertainments 73-80

CHAPTER X.

THE WOMEN OF PARIS—

Housekeeping—Suites of rooms—Little home cooking—The pâtissier—Omnipresent salad—Coffee—The children with their parents—Wives in the business of their husbands—Dress of children—Amusements of children—Toys—The dangers of the streets 81-89

CHAPTER XI.

THE WAYS OF THE FRENCH WORLD—

False impressions of other peoples—Life a movable picture—The activity of French life—Discontent—Temper of the people . 91-96

CHAPTER XII.

THE INVALIDES AND PERE LA CHAISE—

Napoleon's name—The Tomb—The Old Guard—The laws of Napoleon—Woman's rights under the law—The city taxes—The Octroi—Sèvres—The Museum—Pottery . . . 97-104

CONTENTS.

CHAPTER XIII.
THE EIFFEL TOWER—   PAGE
Methods of ascent—Looking down from the first platform—The restaurants—A climb to the next stage—The view—Ascent to the top by the lifts—Looking down—The toy world. . 105–110

CHAPTER XIV.
ORLEANS—
Appearance of the country—The harvest—The streams of water—Farm buildings—Cleanness of town and country—The Maid of Orleans—The Museums—Church of St. Paul—The suburbs 111–118

CHAPTER XV.
BLOIS—
The valley of the Loire—Blois for a time the capital of France—The Catholics and Huguenots—Scenic views—The Chateau—Historical associations 119–126

CHAPTER XVI.
TOURS—
A beautiful garden—The Cathedral—Other historic places round it—Chenonçeaux—Catherine de Medicis—The Chateau—The Inn—Care in railway travelling 127–134

CHAPTER XVII.
NEUCHÂTEL—
Effect of contrasts—The mountains—The river—Social habits 137–142

CHAPTER XVIII.
BERNE—
Picturesque Switzerland—Women on the land—The old houses—The rushing river—The dog as a carrier—The bear symbol 143–148

CHAPTER XIX.
INTERLAKEN—
Its origin—Impressions of the scene—The Hoheweg—The Jungfrau—The dances, gardens, hotels—The contribution to art in the Swiss villages 149–156

CHAPTER XX.
LUCERNE—
The British everywhere—Mount Pilatus—Beauty everywhere in Switzerland—The students on vacation—Lakes of Thun and Brienz—The Giessbach—The excursions on the lake . 157–162

CONTENTS.

CHAPTER XXI.

THE RIGHI—

Ascent by railway—Beauty of the scene—The hotels and pensions —The summit a wondrous picture—The history of Swiss independence 163-170

CHAPTER XXII.

GENEVA—

The memory of Calvin and Voltaire—Voltaire's chapel and tomb —The Museum—The Public Gardens—The University—The city and gardens—The public spirit and history . . 171-178

CHAPTER XXIII.

CHAMOUNIX AND MONT BLANC—

The diligence—Ascents and descents—The majesty of Mont Blanc —The Tête Noire—The gorge of Trient 179-186

CHAPTER XXIV.

LONDON—

A return from Paradise to the commonplace of life—Hard to classify impressions—The rich stores of the Museum—Notable places—Contrasts, rich and poor—Seven Dials—Billingsgate —The Whitechapel district—Philanthropy . . . 189-196

CHAPTER XXV.

LONDON (continued)—

Footsteps of the great—The Temple—The river—Westminster Abbey — Chelsea — The charities — Foundling Hospital— Christ's Hospital—The Charterhouse—Toynbee Hall . 197-203

INTRODUCTION.

THE real traveller, like the true poet, should be born, not made. He should possess within himself certain qualities which would be beyond the power of circumstances to alter, and which would form, so to speak, his spiritual outfit. He should be by nature adaptable, and by grace sympathetic. He should have the power of disentangling himself from the home environment, and of looking upon the differences in custom which belong to other peoples, without that unalterable belief in the superiority of his own which renders one deaf and blind to every advantage. He should possess an eye which has been trained beforehand to some understanding of the beauty and majesty of the natural world, so that he can make comparison of effect, and read the message of sea and sky, valley and mountain-top. He should possess an intelligence somewhat trained by study into a knowledge of the past, so that there shall be a historic background against which the foreground of the visible present may stand in relief. And he should have at least as much good health as is ensured by good digestion and a clear conscience.

It is because these qualities are so frequently omitted, that travel has become the heavy and wearisome pastime it so often is, instead of the inspiration and delight it always should be. Fashion has set its seal upon the habit of wandering: it has become a conventional procedure, with set periods upon which to proceed over set routes, to the accompaniment of set surroundings. Guide-books, instead of inclinations, map the way; expenses are calculated according to the judgment or fancy of others. There is no longer the ardour or desire which makes difficulty vanish; and although the facilities for journeying have increased a thousandfold, they have added in no such degree to the ease and content of the individual. He has grown so accustomed to be cared for and tenderly dealt with, that every molehill of possible inconvenience becomes a mountain of difficulty to fret or fume over. Unprepared, through lack of preliminary training, to make comparison or draw deduction, he resents as a personal affront each enforced violation of his habitual rule of conduct, and makes a grievance of every custom which differs from his own. So that in spite of steam and electricity, of couriers and cooks, of the miracles of art and of science, he returns to his fireside as narrow in mind and as poor in imagination as when he left it.

But to the happy mortal who is dowered with this divine gift of insight, what an age is this in which to enrich existence! There is scarce a spot of the known world which is not open to his enamoured glance; there is no time too short to afford him some precious passing glimpse of beauty, nor too long to be filled with delight to the eye and joy to the understanding. Even moderate circumstance, short of absolute poverty, need not interfere with his desire, if only common sense is allowed to hold the helm of affairs. The cost is made to suit the necessities of so many different incomes, the positive requirements are so small, and the efforts to grade supply so that it may meet every demand so strenuous, that there are few indeed who need deprive themselves wholly of the pleasure of a holiday outing. The will and the way go together.

In the material preparation, whether the pilgrim be one of sentiment or convention, there are certain rules which so simplify routine that they should be considered as axioms. Leaving out of consideration those who are a law unto themselves, who travel with a retinue, and whose bank accounts are so plethoric that a pound is the same thing as a penny, there remains the rank and file of the army of tourists with whom expense is a question, and luggage as much *impedimenta* as it was to the Roman cohorts. The Modern has learned the lesson of its inconvenience as well as the Ancient. Especially in Europe, where the dense fog of ignorance has not yet been dissipated by the sweetness and light of the American check system, it is absolutely matter of necessity to travel in light marching order between places at which no long stay is to be made. In these days of the ever-present shop for every need and fancy under the sun, little more is necessary to be carried about with one than a couple of changes of inner, and one of outer clothing, in case of accident. Any liberal hand-bag will contain these items, especially with the addition of a strap for a rug and warm wrap. Both of these can be lifted into the compartment of the railway train, or the van of the diligence in which their owner is travelling, so that there shall be neither enforced delay nor worry at breaks in the journey. A small satchel suspended from the shoulders or the waist, to hold guide-book, tickets, and purse, will be found a great comfort. Without being clumsy, this could be so enlarged as to hold a simple lunch and a flask of any tonic which one has been accustomed to use in emergencies. With such an outfit, the traveller can be independent of hurried scrambles for stale refreshment at crowded railway stations, and defy any ordinary accident by which he might otherwise be made uncomfortable. It is not an Irish bull, but a simple fact, to say that this statement is doubly true when he happens to be a woman.

As for rules of health and conduct, they are few but imperative: light and easily fitting clothing, simple food taken regularly, a fair amount of sleep, and an understanding that occasional rest must relieve the waste of perpetual motion. Considering the total change which takes place, from the quiet habits which are supposed to be necessary for well-being at home, it is a wonder that more injury does not result in the excitement of journeying. To hurry from a night of broken sleep in railway coach or steamboat to a day of sight-seeing, in which tired eyes grow painfully sensitive from the constant reception of new impressions, and the tired mind becomes languid and irresponsive under the flood of novel experiences, and to continue this indefinitely, is the usual formula. So the zest which should be added to imagination is lost, and the exaltation which might make life rich, degenerates from pure physical weakness into a barren curiosity which endures instead of enjoying. One returns with a chaos of vague remembrances jostling each other in barbaric disorder, instead of a gallery of fair memories in which the soul might sit at ease for ever after.

The ordinary voyager with this little leaven of common sense will at least know comfort, and the tempered pleasure he has a right to expect. His will never be the royal progress of the true Prince, alert of fancy, quick of eye, responsive of spirit, to whom all things offer tribute. But the broadening which unconsciously comes to thought, the breaking down of prejudice, the building up of character, and the sense of re-creation, will remain with him as solace and recompense. Something of the great lesson which is the beginning of a liberal education—the consciousness that " there are more things in heaven and earth than were dreamed of in his philosophy "—has penetrated his understanding, and can never wholly depart. Henceforth he must recognise himself as cousin-german at least, if not brother, to the great family of humanity.

To the real traveller—the royal traveller—one can only say God speed. For him the radiant world waits; and at every turn some new sense of delight comes to make life splendid. Day by day he becomes conscious of heights and depths in his being which were unknown before, until he seems to be for the first time becoming acquainted with himself. In being introduced to this newer and happier self, he revels in the sense of largeness and freedom which the double identity confers upon him. Here are the dreams which have been companions of a lifetime, presenting themselves like the faces of beloved friends for recognition; here is the strong mental exaltation that lingers about the shrines of earth's victories, to make the soul rich with tender emotion as it follows in the path of the immortal brotherhood of spirits. Preferences which had before lain dormant, sensations of which he had never been conscious, draw him this way and that with subtle strength; and he is like one escaping from some denser atmosphere into the purer air and far-reaching enchantment of a diviner world.

That every one who has done her the honour of being for a short time her travelling companion may belong to this blissful company, is the sincere wish of

THE AUTHOR.

THE VOYAGE

A SUMMER HOLIDAY IN EUROPE.

CHAPTER I.
THE VOYAGE.

I WONDER whether there is any room in the world now for the journal of an enthusiast. Mrs. Jameson's Diary of an Ennuyée might have a success; it is an age when the imagination, like the body, must be clothed in pale and faded tints to be in the fashion. How is one going to fare who is out of the mode; who enjoys the high colours and deep reliefs and bright contrasts of primitive nature? Well, we shall see.

Here is a sea voyage, for instance; that old, old story, which has become a nightmare of repetitions and ennui, clouded always with the shadow of sea sickness, full of reminiscences of stuffy small state-rooms and intolerable smells. How is one to be believed who has to paint this as a week of paradise, a succession of balmy days and glorious nights, a revelation of harmonies in colour, in tone, in ensemble, like Mendelssohn's "Calm Sea and Happy Voyage," or like some of those serene motifs of Wagner, which float like dreams of heaven through the discordant harmonies of his "Gotterdämmerung." How is a truthful soul to attempt the chronicle of wrapt and starlit waters, swelling beneath the glory of moons which earth never imagined, pulsing into deep, organ chords of infinite music, which seem to be translated at last into the splendour of the radiant firmament above! Of long, peaceful, blessed days, throbbing with light and the vitality of fresh winds, bearing one through unknown seas to unknown worlds! Of the sensation of belonging to the elements; of being born, somehow, kin to ocean, sky, and air, and being suddenly introduced into companionship with one's relations! And the new thoughts that come knocking at the heart for utterance; the unknown depths that seem to open in the soul for the reception of these unusual emotions; the glamour of unreality that lifts the commonplace out of life and makes existence a strange and novel experience for us.

To sit on the deck of an outer bound ship, the spirit yet throbbing under the unwonted wrench of parting, the eyes yet dim with the pressure of recent tears, and to feel the sweet ministrations of sea and sky interpose their wholesome barrier between the past and the future, is to reach one of the highest points in emotional beatitude which it is ever granted human nature to attain from inanimate causes. The imperceptible, delicious swiftness of motion, the rush of wind and waves, the dazzle and sparkle of light, the sense of buoyancy and unconscious uplift are too strong for expression, but not for feeling. There is an impression of subtle knowledge and strength, of mingled audacity and awe, in thus crossing this beaconless and limitless space, and subordinating the secrets of nature to man's will. The glory is not ours, as it was that of Columbus, to have conceived the thought and turned that first weak prow across the vast unfathomed ocean; yet something of the same divine principle spurs us on. For us, too, there is waiting beyond the happy shore of the new world. For us, too, the dreams and aspirations of a lifetime are about to be accomplished. Timorous fears may cry halt, heart-longings may hale us backward to the safe and quiet homeland we are leaving; but something stronger within—whether it be devil or angel—calls onward now, and we obey the summons.

There is an old Eastern proverb which says, "It is well to be born beautiful; it is better to be born rich; it is best to be born lucky." Surely for some creatures there is such a star in the ascendant. This *Cephalonia*, for instance—not young and lovely, like some of her younger stately sisters, nor endowed with that Atalanta-like swiftness with which they win the flying race with time, yet about whom the waves move tenderly always, and the sky looks down with love. And the happy people aboard her, who leave the dreary uncertainty of early April days, full of doubt and misgiving, prepared for the climate and the costume of the Esquimaux, who find themselves at once in the warmth and glow of the fairest midsummer. Of course they have done something to deserve reward; they have chosen the week of the full April moon, and looked beyond that fatal beauty which is only skin deep in any she that moves, be the same boat or woman. But on the whole they have been irresponsible as babies in their choice. Why, then, should they be so especially blessed in it? Is fortune, like Providence, kind to children and fools?

What an epitome of life is this little world speeding across the great world of waters. What divisions of classes and interests, each having its own sphere—all bound somewhat together by the kindly influences of humanity. The governing order high up on those dizzy bridges, grave with the stern responsibility of active power; the aristocracy of the promenade deck, basking in the sunshine of luxury and idleness; the more numerous and democratic horde gathered into steerage and intermediate quarters; the honourable working body busy about interests and affairs of government, and down deepest of all the silent, grim labourers who work as blindly as the blind machines they tend, but without whom the entire organism would fail. "All sorts and conditions of men" play their part on this small sphere as in the larger one left behind, with just the same mingling of advantages and drawbacks. Sometimes a touch of envy in eyes that look up, and a blank of indifference in those that glance down; sometimes a bit of riotous merry-making on the main deck to mock the well-bred languor of the saloon above it, but as a rule, good, honest, mutual interest one in another. How could it be otherwise when such narrow space and similar conditions limit the present and future for us!

By what miscalculation in the use of words did crossing the ocean ever come to be known as monotonous or tiresome? Of all the adjectives that could possibly be misapplied, how could the one most unfitted of all have been chosen as descriptive? Monotonous, to be born out of the serfdom of custom and the imperious insistance of conventionalities to this wonderful new existence. To be transplanted, like a winter-housed flower, from the pale atmosphere within doors into the jubilation of the air and sunshine; to have an insight into surroundings and emotions of which life has been heretofore as ignorant as if the soul had been born blind. To wake up some morning like this of yesterday, with the smooth surface of the deep gathered into long slopes, white crested, and deep valleys, powdered with snow, while the ship, with new life buoyant in every airy tangle of rope and slender taper of masthead, flies up and down the hills and hollows to a rhythm of beautiful motion as wild and free as the Ride of the Walkyres. To be enveloped in splendours of colour such as seemed to belong only to the glories of revelation — amethyst and beryl, sapphire and emerald, chrysoprase and ruby, glinting and changing from glory to glory under the magic of dawn and of sunset, or the silver glamour of the moon. To hear by snatches the wild minor interludes of the sailors' chorus, swept across the bright or mournful waters; to catch in the dusk fragments of song or story from the picturesque groups on the lower deck, full

always of the pathetic interest of poverty. Or to lie awake
o' night, looking through the handsbreadth of a porthole at
a sea and sky more divine than has ever before been offered
to human eyes; and beyond them with that

> "—— longing,
> That is not akin to pain,"

at the dear faces left behind. Or to descend into the heart of
the ship, into that Inferno of fire and heat from which pulses
the force that fills her veins with life and motion, where wild-
eyed sombre visions, amid a hellish glare of smoke and flame,
feed the open, gaping mouths of the blazing pits about them.
I do not think there is anything in the world so overpowering
in its poetic suggestiveness as this furnace-room in a trans-
atlantic steamer. The time, the place, the uncanny and picturesque circumstances remove it from all other experiences.

Are eight days, or ten, too much for such experiences?
Nay, nor three times ten; if we had not been spoiled first
by that demon of superficiality, which cannot spare time for
more than a passing glance at the fairest sight or deepest
mystery. Unless, indeed, it take on the fashionable form of
a Browning craze or the mysticism of esoteric Buddhism.
And then at last, when looking out in the grey dawn of the
morning in that half glad, half fearful unrest of anticipation
which comes nearing land, one sees the cyclop eye of that
benevolent monster, the lighthouse at Fastnet, flashing its
message of welcome through the silence, what a sudden glow
of thanksgiving and thrill of triumph, as if we, too, had in
some way helped to guide the good ship across a three
thousand mile waste of shifting waters so that she should not
deviate three hundred yards from that one lone rock. Then
and then only one becomes aware of the unconscious effort
which has been underlying the calm satisfaction of this week
of leisure—the tension against which rising wind or straying

cloud or breaking wave has been snapping and straining. Some weight too shadowy to be called dread, too vague for apprehension, slips off the braced shoulders, and a delicious lightness and buoyancy succeeds. It must be purchased, though, by the preliminary passage money; no other coin of the realm can buy its delightsomeness.

Then comes the six or eight hours' sail along the Irish coast—a softer sweetness in the land air blowing through the cordage, a fresher blue in the dazzling waters, a more tender glow in the delicate arching sky. Around the grey Head of Kinsale a pair of fisher boats, with deep red sails, come out to make the morning gladder with their dancing, rocking motions; the low, green hills, and the fair, falling slopes between them, smile a welcome; a cloud of white sea gulls is blown like a drift of snowflakes across the shining sea—so we say our first good morrow to Ireland. When the noisy, fussy little tug comes tumbling like a porpoise to take us away from the majestic and now beloved leviathan, there is a momentary pang, and then a sudden return of the inspiration of enterprise. Now, indeed, and at last the world is before us. With Robert Browning we feel:—

> "The year's at the spring
> And day's at the morn;
> Morning's at seven;
> The hillside's dew pearled,
> The lark's on the wing;
> The snail's on the thorn;
> God's in His heaven—
> All's right with the world."

No one who has a drop of Irish blood in his veins, and who that is fortunate has not, no matter through how many generations of absence it has been filtered, can catch his first near glimpse of this beloved land through the gates of Queenstown Harbour without a thrill of deep and joyful emotion, which will remain among his dearest memories for ever. The inheritance which love has bequeathed, the traditions of song and story, mingle with the exhilaration of again approaching land, and the delight which the great beauty of the scene itself sends thrilling through every vein. The hitherto unknown loveliness of the soft green upon the hills, the vivid masses of golden yellow gorse, shining like decorations upon the brow of height and headland, the sense of perfect quiet after the accustomed rattle of machinery, the soft languor of the warm air, the picturesque lines of grey houses rising from or nestling amid the green slopes, the imposing situation of the fine buildings around which the town is grouped, the massive earthworks and embrasures of the two outlying forts, and the general air of cheerfulness and bright expectancy of the landscape would force the spirit of the least imaginative into sympathy. Once ashore, the impression only deepens; birds are singing blithely on the green boughs; the handsome, straight policeman, with his military air and jaunty good-for-nothing cap glued over his right ear, is courtesy itself in assisting you through the Custom House ordeal; a couple of rattling, fascinating, jaunting cars come up with cheery offer of service. There is an air of good-humoured kindliness about every man, woman, and child within eye and ear-shot, and you are supremely content.

When, later on, one of these same dashing, tipsy little vehicles is whirling you through the country roads about Middleton and Cloyne, satisfaction deepens into royal delight. Around, above, and below, on field and height and deep valley, the wonderful green world lies aglow in the sunshine. Hedges of yellow gorse, like bars of light, intersect the landscape up to the very tips of the rounded hills. The fine, soft, close, emerald carpet is smoothed over a soil that one might imagine had been moulded by some careful hand into perfect evenness. Nature here has outgrown the season of awkwardness and angles; she is all curves, and roundness and grace. She has had time to give to decoration. Not a grey stone wall that is not an enchanting arabesque of mosses, brown and olden, of swaying vine tendrils, of clinging ivy. Not a meadow but is enamelled with tiny pink-tipped daisies, and starred with homely dandelion; not a hedge that is not sweet with the exquisite bloom of small yellow primroses, of pale sprays of blackthorn, of shy purple violets hidden under broad clusters of leaves. Such exuberance of bloom, such chains and wreaths and masses of dainty colour, such a revelling in fair unknown forms of leaf and blossom, is like exploring a new country. Even the birds' voices are different from anything we have remembered. The shrill, clear whistle of the thrush, the carol of the lark, the warble of linnets, the mellow ripple of finches, the song of the blackbird, are unlike the woodland gossip to which we are accustomed. It is a new flood of melody, not less, nor more sweet, but "as one star differs from another in glory." The very forms are unfamiliar; those great, stately crows with their cruel beaks already deep in the corn-fields; those graceful, blue-black jackdaws quarrelling in the middle of a shady boreen; the magpie, rolled alternately in snow and soot; the yellowhammers' golden breasts, the tiny wrens, the small bright robins, even the English sparrows. Here is a walled garden. Espaliered plum and peach trees are trained like vines against the sunny sides, beds of deep flame-coloured wallflowers, mellow with fragrance, great clusters of dark blue forget-me-nots, masses of primroses and marigolds, tall slender stems of monthly roses and massive clumps of flowering shrubs, line the paths and fill the senses with a delicious confusion of scent and colour. In one corner a row of beehives stand in a wilderness of thyme and sweet marjoram, flowering currant and gooseberry bushes, pyramids of Brussels sprouts and long rows of trellised peas. Could honey of Hymettus be more sweetly flavoured than these dripping amber combs, distilled from such riches?

The poetry of pastoral life is in the very air we breathe. Wordsworth becomes suddenly translated for us, and Cowper and Thompson, and Shelley and Tennyson. Here is the muse which inspired them; mild, tender, lovely and loving, instead of the grand, half shy, half savage creature who wanders through the barbaric splendours of American solitudes.

Rory O'Moore, who is driving, is a true son of the soil. He has charged you a shilling too much for the ride, but he has decked your particular chariot with his gayest cushions; he stops to cut armfuls of golden gorse and bouquets of cowslips and anemone; he overflows with good nature, and his rosy face is stretched in a constant smile at the rhapsodies of the "Mericaners." He wears a solid suit of good grey corduroy; there is a sprig of larch stuck into the band of his caubeen, and a bunch of primroses in his buttonhole. "De times is on'y middlin' to be sure, but praise God dere's a hundherd and dirty tousand to be comin' from de oder side dis summer, an' of corse every one dat goes to Paris will be comin' to see how Ireland looks, so we'll be doin' somethin'." "But what makes you think so many are coming?" "Oh, dey tells me so, for gospel trute; an' look now at yereselves, ma'am, comin' so airley in de beginnin' of it all. Sure not a doubt of it." And he cracks his whip reassuringly over the neck of the gaunt but sturdy horse, who is already flying down the steep road in a way to put one's heart in one's mouth. Care and the future are far enough away now, with six good silver shillings in his pocket. Rory isn't one of the pessimists.

The streets of Cork are full of the most alert and businesslike race that I fancy we will meet in the country. Crowds of well dressed, cheery people flow in and out the large, well-filled shops, and saunter through the grounds of Queen's College, or the stately shadows of the Dyke walk later. The city is beautifully situated in the valley of the river Lee and upon the hills on either side. Terraces and crescents of pretty houses, each inside its own high-walled garden, overflowing with leafage and climbing plants, and entered by gates from the street, remind one of Mrs. Oliphant's Green Lane in Carlingford, and add an element of romantic interest to the dwellers therein. Shaggy little Welsh or Kerry ponies, attached to low phaetons filled with rosy-cheeked children, and driven by comfortable, comely matrons, run up and down the steep streets as if each were blown by some concealed steam power. Such spinning around sharp corners and dashing over smooth noiseless pavements was never seen before. Everything is new; bakers' waggons piled high with enormous loaves of bread, queer milk carts, carrying one towering hogshead-like can, char-a-bancs, shandridans, waggonettes, jaunting cars, private equipages, donkey carts, all running at breakneck speed, as if the fate of the nation depended upon post haste. The people seem bitten by a mania for swift motion the moment they touch the reins of a horse. Compared with the easy insouciance of the crowds on the very narrow side-walks, these dashing charioteers are like another people. The shop windows are full of bargains that shake the prudent American soul out of all its resolves against expenditure. What is a man, or especially a woman, to do when Irish mackintoshes can be bought for five or seven dollars, and the finest eider down puffs in the world, cased in silk or in satin, for fifteen? The consistent he or she who prays "Lead us not into temptation" should keep clear of Cork.

IRELAND.

CHAPTER II.

GLENGARIFF AND KILLARNEY.

BEFORE one has been a day in Ireland, a certain number of strangenesses, where all is strange, impress themselves. One is the omnipresence of the military element. The peaceful stranger, to whom the pomp and circumstance of this phase of human nature is unknown, fancies himself in the midst of war preparations. Red-coated privates on the side-walks; stately officers in dog-carts, on horseback, or afoot; companies and squads going through drills in barrack yards; and barracks themselves, of infantry, of cavalry, of artillery, of constabulary, everywhere in town and country, up hill and down dale. Partly the splendid setting up of military training, partly the conscious and acknowledged importance of their position, gives these men an air of arrogance, or at least of condescension, which produces a sentiment of awful respect in the ordinary mortal. One feels as if revolution were in the air, and that at the next corner the troops with drums beating and colours flying will go marching by to the seat of war. But no! There is no war and no enemy. There is no *raison d'etre* so far as common sense can reach. But common sense has so little to do with the government of nations.

By the time one has rambled about for ten days or a fortnight this effect of surprise vanishes. It becomes the most natural thing in the world to look for the comfortable police headquarters in the prettiest part of every town or village, or in the most imposing position in the approach to a city.

One forgets to wonder what they are for, or what possible occupation they can find on these quiet green highways and byways, so full of peace and restfulness. One forgets even to dread the possibilities of misfortune and evil which these numbers of able-bodied and idle men, passing their time in aimless manœuvres under enforced regulations, may represent to the communities upon which they are imposed. When, now and again, one to the manner born attempts an explanation, it seems easier to remain within the safe shield of what the Catholic Church calls "impenetrable ignorance." What! a Government constantly holding its place over its people by force! Not a sudden uprising in gusty passion over some real or fancied injustice, but a constant, undying, desperate protest against authority! This authority imposed upon instead of appointed by them! As poor Stephen says in "Hard Times," "It's aw' a muddle." Let us leave it so.

Almost as perplexing is the endeavour to grasp the idea that the whole visible earth is the personal property of this or that individual. It does not belong to the peasant who makes his little field teem with plenty; nor to the farmer whose broad lands stretch in pasture and wheat land and garden up the beautiful slopes; nor even always to the gentleman whose smiling villa fits upon its sunny height, or into its shady glen, as if it were part of the natural order. It is the domain of some man or woman, who lives upon the revenue of its bounty in other lands, who never sees or knows it, except for a few weeks of shooting or fishing in the season, and to whom it means only so much rent in pocket. Now and again in the most lovely portions of the scenery a high stone wall cuts off the view of lake or mountain for miles, and one moves as if in a city street, able to look only above and before one. The owner who shuts you out from your share of the glory of the world in this way, is not even enjoying it himself. He is the absentee in London or Paris, and "he does what he likes with his own." His is the mountain yonder with its head lost in the clouds; his the lake reflecting the smile of heaven; his the river flowing through its tranquil meadows. You climb the height or sail the waters, you fish in the stream or hunt in the covert, only by his permission. No wonder that in time he becomes such a representative of the power of the Almighty to the crowd of lesser folk who hang upon his will. If only *noblesse oblige* should be always his motto! If partaking some of His attributes, he would also share His mercy and loving-kindness. But the miserable cabins of the people answer that!

Still another peculiarity—to the American—is the stamp which royalty leaves upon whatever it touches. The Prince of Wales, when a youth of seventeen, travelled with his tutor over the beautiful Glengariff country between Bantry and Killarney. Tens of thousands of more illustrious and splendidly endowed men have traversed it since, people whose names and fortunes have been more closely linked with the glory of the land than any accident of birth or position could rivet them, yet loyalty has called it the Prince of Wales route from that day to this, and no doubt will continue to do so. That simple little lodge has been sacred among all its richer and braver brethren because once the Queen lunched under its roof; another point is hallowed in that some Royal Highness professed himself pleased with the outlook. Compared with such prestige as this, Ruskin could confer no patent of nobility on height or depth. King of the mountains though he be, the material sovereignty of the rulers of the land is higher and prouder than his in the minds of the people. But we must leave this pregnant theme for a look at happier things.

The journey from Bantry to Glengariff, and thence on to Killarney, allowing a few days for rest and enjoyment in the middle passage, is as exquisite an experience as the heart of man could desire. Taken in one of the high, strong mountain coaches, open all around, and well provided with rugs even in summer, it is a dream of beauty. But the halcyon time is in early May. The season matches our early June weather. There is that look of new creation about the world; that infinite tenderness and delicacy in the young frail boughs, the springing grass, the glad field flowers, the singing bird voices. But what boughs and grass and flowers! What tints and blooms unknown to us before; what garlanding of ivy; what wonders in hedge and roadside. The beautiful quaint grey houses, with their bright unshuttered windows, are close covered with clinging leaves from foundation to gable; the plantations of young larches are tremulous, like a shower of translucent emerald light; the gorse-covered cliffs shine like solid gold in the sunshine; the cultivated fields creep to the tip of the hill slopes in an arabesque of gracious greens and warm greys. Here a tumbling stream turns the shining black wheel of an old mill; there the ivy-robed tower of some ancient ruin gladdens the valley; Gray's country churchyard lies amid its black yews and mossy graves under the shadow of its village spire; Goldsmith's Sweet Auburn waits you at the turn of yonder road where the grassy stile leads across the meadows to the hamlet beyond. And now the cliffs rise and the seaward mountains; the salt breath of the waves mingles with the scent of violet and primrose; the clouds come scurrying down from the west, and a pelting shower rattles about your ears, to be up and off again the next moment. The sun is out anew with an added dazzle and lustre for its momentary eclipse; the birds rush into a more riotous tangle of melody; the flowers actually laugh in the hedges; a fresh set of pictures roll past in the panorama of light and loveliness; the dim, blue, far away mountains begin to show on the horizon, and it is time for another shower. No one minds it. A sane person is never unprovided with a waterproof and umbrella; there is no sting in the air to make a wetting uncomfortable; it is all generous, kindly, hospitable, and fascinating, like the people to whom it belongs.

Glengariff itself is a gem. Skirting the edge of the deep bay, surrounded by bold headlands and craggy mountain peaks, it nestles amid its fields, removed from the turmoil of the outside world as if it never belonged to it. Down on the shore, sheltered by an abrupt hillside behind, Eccles Hotel waits for the traveller. It is the dearest and quaintest little inn. A long, low house, with two irregular higher wings at the sides, and other larger additions in the background, covered to the eaves with a climbing mass of vines and roses and clematis and blue lupin, banked with clusters and beds of every dainty flower, it is so completely hid in its veil of green and wreaths of blossoms that one has to guess at the original colour beneath. It is the most tempting hostelry. On the steps of the low, wide hall door the landlady meets you with ready welcome, a sturdy mountain lad shoulders your luggage, a neatly capped and aproned maid takes the number of your room from the kindly woman clerk and ushers you upstairs; there are flowers on your table, and a chintz valance to the neat little bed. You are quite at home. A tidy woman comes to know what you would like for dinner, and to suggest some tit-bit for which the house is famous. You are led downstairs again to be introduced to the drawing-room, full of flowers and small tables, and easy chairs, and the universal antimacassar, with deep windows looking out through clustering vines at the lake. You are shown through one long, mysterious passage to the library, low and bright, and so quiet—a dusky little nest for lounging and reading; back again and through another winding way to the dining-room, with its four bay windows opening into the flower garden, and garlanded in green; its little and big tables gay with great pots of Cineraria in luxuriant bloom; its sideboards dainty with precious bits of Sevres and Doulton, and bright with old silver; its walls completely covered with old pictures, family portraits, copies of celebrated canvases and originals, some valuable, some dreadful. The house is full of angles and corners; passages upstairs and passages down, unforeseen niches and cupboards, and a collection of bric-a-brac that would fill a museum. The hot and cold joints are brought in whole for breakfast, and carved to your taste on a side table; the matron pours your cup of only passable coffee, but delicious tea, from the urn; the great loaf of bread is given into your own hands to cut. Little pats of creamy butter —was or will there be ever again such in the world as this of Cork—are at your plate; a slice of broiled plaice fresh from the bay, a rasher of bacon, a fresh egg or a salmon steak. This is the whole, but it is so good, so homelike, that it never occurs to one to require greater variety any more than if it were your friend's table. It is your friend's table—or your own. The element of personal interest and kindliness is so strong in the service offered, that you feel yourself part of a family, not portion of a crowd. There is not the machine-like perfection of the Windsor or the Palmer House, where anything within the compass of the earth can be laid at your feet by touching an electric knob inside your door, but there is something more human, more pleasing.

Outside the porch a hedge of fuchsias, three feet high and quite three feet wide, divides the house front from the narrow country road; the blue sea breaks among the rocks just across it; little boats with gay burdens of pleasure-seekers float in and out among the sunny islands. The small, clean windows look out from a compact mass of flowers and foliage, bright with every known tint; wallflowers and primroses make the sweet air sweeter; gravelled paths wind here and there up the hillside, through wildernesses of bloom and fragrance, laurustinas and rhododendron, clumps of laburnums and sombre yew shadows. Thatched summer houses and rustic seats are in every nook, each with its especial ravishment of view, and the air is absolutely tipsy with melody. The Irish birds are like its people, bubbling over with song and laughter. And over and above all is an air of peace, of content, of satisfied remoteness from care and bustle that was never felt before. Yet in this same precious inn there are lapses that would make a Western hotelkeeper's hair stand on end. There is lack in the little bedrooms, of many conveniences and most luxuries. The housemaid sweeps her halls and stairs at nine o'clock in the morning with a fine free motion, driving clouds of dust into the guests' faces without a word of apology. Your bath is a pail of warm water in a tin tub; you go to bed with a candle; the men and maids chatter and laugh outside your door frankly, boisterously—if you desire to sleep, so much the worse for you.

Such happy days as one spends here threading the wood-paths, exploring the gorse-covered glens, rambling through the mazes of Lord Bantry's hunting ground, with its picturesque thatched shooting lodge, visiting the ruins of Cromwell's bridge, climbing the battlements of the Martello, on one of the outlying islands. This is one remnant of a bit of folly perpetrated by some rattle-brained patriot at the time when the first Napoleon hovered like a war cloud over the sky of Europe. A number of these massive structures were erected on different exposed points along shore to prevent any sudden invasion by the French troops. They would have been about as much obstacle to Bonaparte's plans as a five-barred gate to an athlete; but the erratic genius who planned them deserves the thanks of posterity for the beauty they add to the sea line here and there. We found ours with a barefooted urchin as warder, who threw open the postern gate for a silver shilling; and garrisoned by a tiny black kid, who came scampering down the broken wall to butt at the approaching enemy.

The drive of forty miles from Glengariff to Killarney is exceedingly beautiful. One is not prepared for the boldness and great wildness of the mountain passes, or for the scowling majesty of the mountains themselves, rising in black drifted billows of rock 3000 feet against the sky, frowning under the sudden eddies of shadow, which even on the fairest day sweep about their gorges and precipices. The loveliest network of cultivated fields creeps everywhere like a soft rug to the very foot of the mountain across the wide sunny valleys; the grey stone cabins, with their thatched roofs, fit into clefts of the rock, and their sylvan following of a cow, a goat or two, half a dozen sheep, and a shaggy donkey, browse in the sheltered bits of pasture. It is the most perfect blending of pastoral gentleness and savage nature; one intensifies the force of the other. There is a noticeable absence of trees, except in the more immediate vicinity of some proprietor's residence, through all this south-western portion of Ireland. Here and there a plantation of young larches on a hillside or on a portion of a reclaimed bog lends a dainty touch of colour to the fierce grey black of the background; the parks of the large domains have some magnificent specimens of oak, pine, fir, or beech, singly and in groups, with here and there stately avenues leading to fine groves; but the country as a whole is bare except for the always beautiful and luxuriant shrubbery. One is scarcely conscious of any want, surrounded by this exquisite richness of emerald grass, these ever wonderful hedges of privet, of fuchsias, of hawthorn, of shining ivy; that luxuriance of bloom and verdure enamelling every spot upon which the eye rests. No wild flower can compare for daintiness with this pale and fragrant primrose, which is almost as omnipresent in spring as the sod from which it rises; and the pink-tipped star of the lovely wee daisy presses it close. The cowslip is exquisite too, and the violet—all changed into forms rarer and fairer than we across the water have known them.

Killarney, unlike Glengariff, does not take one by storm with its beauty. So many traditions of the charm of this place belong to memory that it takes some time to adjust one's impressions. But it creeps quickly into the heart, and finds there the niche prepared for it. Like the district through which one passes to reach it, there is a fascinating combination of majesty and loveliness. The bright waters and verdant islands look smiling up from the shadow of dark storm-ribbed hills, stern in purple splendour of deep colour, lifting their bare brows to the changeful heavens, with an aspect of solemnity and savage power one could not expect from their height. The entire country side is full of the most enchanting walks and drives. The lovely ruin of Muckross Abbey, with the monks' cloister still in wonderful preservation, and a superb yew tree, seven hundred and fifty years old, growing in the centre of the arched quadrangle, is one of the most impressive. A week can be passed with great delight among new objects of interest each day. Here as everywhere else each spot is memorable because at some one time "the Queen tuk the water here, my lady," or "the Prince looked at the view from this very windy," or "Her Majesty herself clumb up this path, ma'am, an' planted this oak wid her own hand. So it's called the ro'il oak to this day." And it is this country and this people, loyal even to a name and a memory, faithful to some forlorn thought of devotion, that Her Majesty looks upon with such supreme distrust and scant courtesy.

When you go to Killarney let us hope you will stop at the Lake Hotel; that there will be a good fire in the drawing-room, fresh salmon and lake trout "that were swimmin' there before your eyes this morning, madam," on the breakfast table, and that fine old butler, with the air of an earl, behind your chair to serve them. Let us hope, too, that there will be only enough cloud in the sky to cast the proper shadows on gloomy Torc and lonely Mangerton; that the lovely island of Innisfail may glow in the soft sunshine; the pale blue range of the Dingle mountains fade away like clouds in the southern sky; and that there may be a pair of Irish sportsmen to the fore, with mighty calves and brawny arms—brave Nimrods and great trencher men. Above all, let us trust that you may grow accustomed to my Lord Kenmare and my gentleman Herbert asking a fee before they allow you to look upon park or pleasure ground, river or waterfall, mountain or valley. Is it not all theirs, to do what they please with; and in a country where the beggar stretches his poor hand for a penny, why may not the gentle be allowed to stretch his itching palm for the shilling? It will be a blow to your republican prejudices. But by this time you have received enough delight from this lovely and kindly land to bear a few slaps. Besides, it is not the real Ireland that gives them.

CHAPTER III.

DUBLIN AND ITS SUBURBS.

COMING to Dublin after London is like reaching a centre of kindly sympathies, where abstract intelligence is more modified by human warmth, and the atmosphere is at once less brilliant and less mean than above its step-sister capital. The sanguine Celtic temperament robs even poverty of the oppressive ugliness which makes its rags and tatters so inexpressibly repulsive in England; and although the misery may be just as extreme, it is less hideous. The vital interest of the people in the absorbing political interests of the hour gives an alertness and vigour to the physical as well as mental aspect which reminds one more of American processes. The city itself is a wholesome-looking, well-built city, with one really splendid and many fine thoroughfares, and with a series of really attractive suburbs filled with the homes of its prosperous business men. These pretty houses, each in its own bit of garden, with low grey walls and fanciful clumps of shrubbery shutting them from the eyes of the passer-by, hidden like nests among their vines and trellises, have an individuality one would not think possible with such uniformity of construction. They are mostly of two stories, the first being developed as a sort of basement, and the second carrying the visitor up a long flight of steps to the hall door. Each has its own attractive name on the post of the garden gate, telling the passer-by that this is Rose Cottage, and that Shanley Villa, and the other Wellington House. Tramways, as they call our horse cars, with seats on the roof as well as inside, pass in every direction; and the charge of a penny seems ridiculously low. There are numberless handsome squares, some kept in order by the town, some owned by the abutters, who use them as playgrounds for the children or tennis courts for the elders. The kindly climate lends itself to their adorning, and the most wonderful lawns cover them to the hedges of hawthorn. The habit of building directly upon the ground, without the interposition of any proper foundation or cellar, cannot add either to health or comfort in such a wet climate, but the rich counteract the effect by fires in all the different rooms after a very cheery and comfortable fashion, while the poor accept the rheumatism and low fevers engendered as coming from the hand of God and a discipline not to be questioned. There are more crimes committed by human ignorance in His name than even in that of Liberty.

The courtesy of the shop-people, even in a more marked degree than France and England, is in striking contrast to the ill-bred rudeness of our home product. It is a pleasure to buy from these courteous and attentive salesmen, and one hungers for the time when such a system shall have been imported with Irish frieze topcoats and Pims' poplins. The firm that first adopts it is predestined to success. The vulgarity of the tradespeople in most American stores is positively offensive, and to one who has ever tasted the comfort of the Old World regime its very remembrance is intolerable.

The wonderful neatness of the butchers' shops is another national characteristic; and the dainty way in which joints, cuts, and poultry are sent home certainly lends zest to appetite. The greengrocers' stands, as they call provision dealers, are bright with masses of flowers interspersed among the vegetables, and the effect is wholly pleasing. Some of the favourite combinations, such as chicken and bacon, or pork and greens, remind one of the South; the flavours of all the varieties are more rich and delicious than our own, especially that of the cauliflower. Prices of every kind are much lower than those to which we have been accustomed. In clothes for men and boys, cloth garments and personal furnishings generally, it would seem as if a large family might be brought to Dublin, fitted with all the necessaries for a year's outfit, and taken back to America for less than the mere cost of the articles at home. It is quite impossible to resist the fever of purchasing. One buys, and buys, and buys.

And meantime one goes rambling about down the fine expanse of Sackville Street, with Nelson's Pillar and its attendant groups of statuary as landmarks, among them that celebrated bronze figure of the nation's poet, of which some local wag once wrote in relation to its black colour—

"'Tis not Tom Moore, but the Moor of Venice."

One wanders into the historic old House of Parliament, now degraded to the uses of the Bank of Ireland, with the fine tapestries of its House of Lords and the magnificent proportions of its House of Commons. One feels in anticipation the thrill of triumph with which the people will welcome "their own again" to the scene of their former glory, and recognises the intensity with which that day is anticipated by the patient but determined race which has never given up its claim to the right of self-government. When the fashion in which the Irish have been withheld from the exercise of free will is recognised by the traveller, when he comes everywhere upon evidences of the repression and distrust which have been their portion for generations, many things become plain to him which before were obscure. Bolts and bars upon every gate to keep out or hold in; walls about every morsel of property as if there were no moral force beyond to prevent depredation or ensure security; barracks of constabulary stationed at the entrance of every town sufficiently flourishing to be raised above the appearance of mediocrity, and an attitude of suspicion maintained toward every expression of feeling—how can any other result than that of reprisal, or any state of feeling than that of aggravation, be engendered? It is but human to repay injustice of sentiment with depravity of conduct; and it is to the everlasting credit of the nation that it has held its natural passion so well in check, as its record for the past years can show. What it will be when the era of approaching goodwill dawns upon its fortunes, and the sweet, strong light of justice smiles upon its ardent and grateful nature, it is pleasure to think upon.

The reverence with which the people cling to old customs and servants is shown in the bank-note printing of this same institution, where an ancient and groaning engine, with a fly wheel large enough to turn a factory upside down, and only strong enough to move one or two presses, is still retained in its former service. It is kindly remembrance and not economy which leaves it in its place, from which we would have sold it for old iron forty years ago. The same tenderness for old memories is shown in Trinity College, where every eccentricity of the early foundation is still observed. It is a fine old place, with its portraits of bewigged and powdered worthies from Queen Elizabeth down, its treasures of rare old books and manuscripts, its beautiful quadrangle and magnificent library. Looking at the wonderful hand-wrought manuscripts, enriched with illuminations still brilliant with colour, and so artistically perfect that it resembles the daintiest copperplate in the shape and exactness of its lettering, one begins to realise more strongly than ever before that this is indeed the Old World. A volume handed down from the seventh or eighth century! Pages touched lovingly and longingly by hands that have been dust and ashes for a thousand years! And we who look upon them, exponents of a land and a civilisation unknown for more than seven hundred years after they had passed for ever! What slender and frail figures we are, immature children of the dawn, compared with that robust and vigorous existence. The strange old hall used as Commons, where the boisterous collegians assemble daily for dinner, looks as if it too had descended from the Middle Ages. Such dingy, battered tables; such well-used greasy benches; such an undescribable smell of stale puddings and cold roast beef; one does not know whether the odour of sanctity or of victuals is strongest. The chapel is very fine, with beautiful stalls of carved oak for the Dean and Faculty, a very ornate organ, and queer reading desks and chairs for the choir leaders. The whole college has a dim mysterious air, half age, half mustiness, which is worth its weight in gold for any one with a proper bump of veneration.

Between the showers some fine day—for it is always vibrating between rain and sunshine—there are lovely spots to be seen outside the city limits, among the delectable mountains of Bray, or the fair hill of Howth. If you can choose your time, the walks and drives about Killiney and Bray will deservedly live in memory. Take a day more than usually turbulent and spasmodic; have a flat, low light reflected under a grey cloud hanging over the water which breaks along the wide esplanade on the strand; see the cosy little town with Lord Meath's model cottages and cottagers in the same chiaro-oscuro which brings out the soft colours of the landscape to perfection; let a whirling storm of wind and rain seize you on the ascent to Bray Head, driving grey sheets of fog from the tossing Atlantic over its black ledges and dun furze bushes, and howling with a noise like thunder around the foam-showered rocks at the base. Then turn a sharp corner, and order the sunshine to fall upon the fair valley of the Dargle, with its sweet peaceful fields, with its background of blue Wicklow Mountains, and its enchanted castle lying amid bright lawns and parks just below; so exquisitely set in picturesque remoteness that it recalls all the ballads of old romance while still leaving you wedded to reality. After that it may hail or snow, smile or rage, as it pleases. Your picture has been set in its niche in the gallery of memory, and there it will remain to enrich you. But if it should be rain, and it probably will, call at one of the small confectioners in the town; have a cup of hot coffee and a couple of well-buttered toasted crumpets; draw your small table up to the fireside with your feet on the fender in the atom of a back parlour; have a couple of stout cheery friends on the opposite side of the hearth—and you need not call the king your uncle. For that day at least you are above any happenings of fate.

Throughout the land both in town and country there are the strangest reminiscences of Mexico. No place could be more thoroughly unlike in its main characteristics, covered as it is with such witchery of green, and showing everywhere such evidences of cultivation. Mexico is a grey desert, with here and there an oasis of verdure; Ireland is a necklace of emerald, with scarce a vestige of the setting. But here as there the small shaggy donkeys trot about the narrow roads with their heavy creels of strange merchandise, mountains of turf instead of fagots, rising above their patient ears; the winding lanes pass between high grey or white walls, with no break beyond an occasional garden gate; and the small, low, one-story houses, almost blank except for the tiniest windows and a boarded door, turn their prettiest face inward to the little back gardens. Above all, and saddest of all, it too is cursed with the shadow of the absentee landlord, coming for ever between it and the sun of prosperity, with the interposition of the resident agent between principals and dependants. Something of the forlornness which always made itself felt even amid the wonderful beauty of that radiant southern land is here too. And something in the pathetic eyes of the poor and the children, though these are Irish blue instead of the mellow Spanish darkness; and the cheeks of tawny olive there, glow rosy red under this softer sun. It gives an odd sensation of unreality to note such likenesses amid such differences, like a transmigration of souls, for here too is the sad mystery of oppression.

It would be hard to find any city more active in charity and the interest of its citizens in every form of progressive reform. Of hospitals alone there are twenty-eight, besides many public dispensaries, and in only one, the Adelaide, is there any sectarian bias. Different forms of associated benevolent and educational works are conducted with great earnestness and unflagging devotion. Nor is it less zealous in the mental activity which flowers into written and spoken speech in its multitude of literary, scientific, and political clubs. In one of these, gathered informally to meet Mrs. Humphrey Ward, I heard one night as keen and brilliant a discussion upon the relations between Christianity and morals as it has ever been my lot to listen to. In choice of language, force of argument, keenness of analysis and fluency of English speech, it leads my memory of artistic evenings. The number of students, thinkers, and workers one meets in society forms a splendid proportion of the numerical population, and cannot fail to colour one's remembrance. Socially the atmosphere is most delightful, with a generous warmth that brightens all its best qualities.

Midway across the country from Dublin to Killarney, on the line of the Great Southern and Western Railway, one passes through what used to be known as the Golden Valley, from the richness of its wheat lands, but which, though still largely cultivated, has lost much of its renown in this regard. One passes also what might be called the coal mines of Ireland—enormous peat fields, or bogs, black, covered thickly with furze, and pitted everywhere with water. The dried fuel gives an intense but short-lived heat, and is very largely used by the country people. Although it belongs to the wildest portions of the land, the right to cut it must still be purchased by peasants and farmers desiring to avail themselves of the privilege. This principle, that nothing belongs to the people; that they cannot ride or ramble, fish or shoot, sow or reap, except by lease or license of some higher authority, is a difficult lesson for a stranger to learn. What must it be for those who are obliged to know it by heart? Never absolutely to own the little house which shelters one and is endeared by home association; to plant one's trees, tend one's flowers, expend one's labour on improvements which by-and-by, in one year, in ten, in fifty, in a hundred, will revert from your posterity to that of your landlord,—how does this leave heart for hope or perseverance? Other causes may, many others absolutely do, complicate the solution of public questions in Ireland, but this is at the head and root of the offending. There is something in the essence of human nature which rebels against regular industry in such a case. Laws have been passed within the past few years, obliging the owner of property to take into consideration the improvements of his tenant; but up to that time even a coat of whitewash on a cabin wall was sufficient cause for an increase of rent. There will need to be a higher law still of natural justice for the poor man before the problem demonstrates itself.

FRANCE.

CHAPTER IV.

FIRST IMPRESSIONS OF PARIS.

As certainly as the Irish and English landscapes suggest the characters of the people to whom they belong, does the country portion of France reflect the traits of the race that occupies it. There is more irregularity, more individuality, as if each small field belonged to the person who tilled it, instead of being only a portion of some larger plan. There is no such appearance of wealth and state collected about a few great houses; and the cottages of the peasantry are almost invariably gathered into close groups, as if a stronger tie of interest and kindliness bound the occupants to each other. The trees are not so beautiful, but they are more diverse. There is more colour dashed in here and there. Red-tiled roofs, mellowed into warmer and deeper tints by time and creeping verdure, shine among the stiff Normandy poplars or the softer foliage of the orchards; and each holding, however small, seems to embrace within its limits all the different necessaries for the comfort of the household. One is planted wholly with corn, and another with beans, and a third with potatoes; each is a separate little market-garden, neat and trim, with flowers sprinkled among the vegetable-beds, and every inch of room made useful.

Over and over again one passes just such quiet churches, with the village churchyard nestled about it, and the Curé's house in its walled garden close by, as make the story of the Abbé Constantin delightful. Men in blouses, women in blue aprons, with heavy thick shoes that are a weight to carry, tramp through fields and lanes, digging, weeding, planting, seldom—it is very seldom—resting. But this is not new. The English and Irish fields had this point in common with them. After all, I think the hardship of this outdoor work for women is more in fancy than reality. It must be taken into consideration that there is very little household care to occupy the time or sap the strength of these wives and daughters of the peasantry. There is, likewise, no sense of degradation or unusual poverty attaching to it; the women-folk of the farmer, as well as those of his labourer, take part. It is a question whether those so engaged are not healthier and happier than many of our own well-to-do farm-women, whose overworked lives are passed inside the house, with its always darkened windows, away from fresh air and sunshine, and with a thousand petty details, required by custom rather than common-sense, to keep them for ever in arrears. It is not the work absolutely required by her circumstances which breaks the heart and health of so many American women in the country districts, but the exigencies of dress for herself and her children, the plenishing of her unhealthfully profuse table and storeroom, the conforming her days to the customs of those about her. In those cases there is almost as strong an obligation of caste with us as among the Hindoos. This strain upon nerves and time the French peasant wholly avoids. A woollen dress and stout jean apron; a cap for Sunday and *fête*, and no head-gear at all for the rest of the week; an equally limited and serviceable wardrobe for husband and children—there is nothing in this to break down from worry. And the brown bread, the salad of any green thing that grows, the *pot-au-feu*, with its savoury stew, the milk and butter from the only cow, the fresh eggs and vegetables,—still, there is nought to weigh heavily upon time or engross attention too severely. It is primitive, of course; but primitive things have their uses and conveniences, as well as complex. In view of the ever-increasing mountain of mental troubles which threaten the health and happiness of our own country with its avalanches, it might be well to study some other methods of life. These people, if poor, are yet wholesome, happy, and contented. If higher civilisation, with all its delights and compensations, is going to deny us these gifts of the gods, we should try some other experiments.

In the whole wide world can there be anything like the dazzle and glamour of Paris, for the stranger who comes for the first time within its gates ? Afterward there may be greater understanding of the charm, deeper insight into the springs whence this enchantment of soul and sense flows; but can anything ever equal the delicious intoxication which seizes one standing for the first time in the centre of this whirl of life and gaiety ? Before one knows the meaning of these wonders which gladden the vision; before one remembers the historic glories which have lent a soul to the inanimate splendour which surrounds him ; while the brain is still dizzy from the changeful, brilliant tumult, and the eyes yet blinded by the unaccustomed airiness and brightness ! Take the Place de la Concorde on a summer morning, with that wonderful avenue of the Champs Elysées stretching on to the Arc de Triomphe. The early clouds have floated away from the laughing sky; the broad leaves of the chestnut trees are swaying in the warm sunshine ; a mob of carriages, airy, light, reflecting the sun's rays from polished surfaces with every turn of the wheel, skims over the smooth pavement of the great central space. Cavalcades of splendidly mounted equestrians dash up and down the roadways prepared for them under arching greenery; a world of brilliantly dressed people fill the four side-walks, each wider than most of our streets, with rapid, flashing motion. Over the vast playground little children are sitting, running, walking; fountains fling glistening spray of silver waters high in air; flowers are blooming in great beds of fragrance and beauty; a company of red-trousered infantry, with a military band in front, come marching down the central distance. Compared with the broad-shouldered giants across the Channel, they look like toy-soldiers. One is forced to remember the tremendous record they have left written in blood on the battlefields of Europe before being able to associate them with any idea of force. As it is, they harmonise better with the glad and stirring scene of which they make part. What has thought of strife or death to do with this gay fantasia of life and colour? Breasting this tremendous outpouring of sound, brilliancy, and motion, the strong silence of the beautiful groups of statuary placed about the great square has an artistic value it could never reach elsewhere. The mourning wreaths and crosses surrounding the memorial from Alsace and Lorraine, constantly renewed by loyal hands, lend a touch of purely French sentiment to one of the details of the picture. The great Egyptian monolith in the centre adds its dash of Oriental expression to the spectacle; under its shadow, at any hour one chooses, there pass burnoosed Arabs, turbaned Moslems, representatives of every race and power on the face of the globe, until one ceases to be surprised at anything that happens. At one side, under the light arches of the bridges, dart long slight boats, crowded with passengers, like glistening water-flies shooting over the clear shining waters. At another, the fine Greek façade of the Madeleine ennobles the vista which it completes with its solemn beauty; the gardens of the Tuileries hide with their loveliness the scars beyond them left by torch and axe of the Commune on that memorable May day eighteen years ago. But why bring image of destruction into this atmosphere? Neither it, nor death, nor sorrow, nor pain, has any place in this glad *ensemble*. The scene is for the comedy of life, not its tragedy.

Then—still before the newness wears away, and that happy sense of irresponsibility which takes what presents itself without any after-thought of what it meant in the past or presages for the future—turn in any direction, and let the essence of the place mount like some subtle elixir into your brain, and set the pulses beating. See the long, wide, lovely streets, almost as clean as those of Mexico, stretch far into the distance, lined with stately rows of palaces, set in gardens, which glow and brighten behind their wrought-iron railings. Down the centre always the constant stream of carriages, with the quiet liveries of the very rich, the more gorgeous outfit of the *bourgeois gentilhomme*, the shining hat and scarlet waistcoat of the professional coachman. One begins to understand a phrase of which French writers make constant use in describing an attractive house. These are all "*maisons coquettes.*" There is coquetry in the long windows, lace-veiled, opening like doors upon the pretty iron balconies; coquetry in these dainty footholds for lounging and observation, carried through every story, filled with flowers and plants, shaded here and there by fanciful awnings; coquetry in the glimpses of inner courts caught through wide arches leading from the side-walk, and bright with shrubbery and fountains. Each turns an animated face to the street, greeting the outside world with a smile, but it reserves a special glance for its intimates. It is as near the human attribute as inanimate nature can ever come.

Or turn toward the business quarter. Note the glittering windows of the small shops—for, with a few exceptions, they are all small, unlike our caravansaries. The Maison Aristide-Boucicaut, as they call the Bonne Marché, the

Magazin du Louvre, and a few others recall our American dimensions, but these are all. And even these are so different. Such courtesy, such groupings of colour and effect, such facility for choice, above all such bargains! But we must leave this tempting particular discussion for another time, and return to the general subject. Every rare and exquisite thing known to the refinement of this earth is here in its highest perfection. Such fans and jewels and trinkets, such toys and porcelain and bronzes, such variety of daintinesses for decoration and delight! And such quantities of everything! If all the countries were rich, and all had come here to spend their riches, could they do more than keep this world's fair in progress? Is there any provision for the poor; is there any note made of their necessities; is there any chance for them in this marvellous pleasure-ground of refinement and wealth? Are there any poor left to care for?

Turn this other corner and answer for yourself. A franc, as you know, is twenty cents, and a franc is made up of a hundred centimes. Here are parcels of vegetables, bits of meat, plates of cooked food, well-seasoned broths, minute divisions of bread and butter, of fruits and seasonings, from a couple of centimes to a gros sous, which equals ten. If the franc were actually a dollar it could scarce have more purchasing power, and certainly not at all the variety of provisions to choose from, which it has here. Everything is wholesome and inviting: the beneficent omnipresence of legal supervision enforces the one; the native tact and taste of the people supply the other. Instead of one heavy and tasteless mass, the poor man as well as the rich can have his savoury and appetising morsels; and this on the basis of a fifth part of a cent, upon which, as being its lowest coin, French values are built. Here, too, are the materials for the simple clothes, the blouse, the apron, the woollen gown, the heavy pantaloon, the child's plain, substantial dress. So infinitely cheap are they, according to our standard, that one is mute with astonishment. Here are amusements, circuses, theatres, panoramas, side-walk *cafés*. Here are omnibuses and tramways, going for next to nothing into the green fields and country lanes. Here are military bands playing at evening in the great Squares and wide Places; and the great Squares and Places themselves, the most exquisite and beautiful on earth, made glad with fountains and flowers, glorious with statues and monuments, filled with brightness by day and night, all for the poor man and the poor man's children. At least he is as welcome there as his master, and he has the consciousness of his right.

If he has a love for art, what a paradise is here opened to him! Outside and in, these public buildings are such marvels. The eye most untrained in technicalities must still become accustomed through habit to recognise the good and the true in proportion as well as execution. One can imagine the heart-hunger which Boston, or New York, or Chicago, would leave in a nature accustomed to this outlook. Everything seems to have been planned with a view to beauty. The common street fountains, which are always artistically pleasing, and sometimes of wondrous elegance, like that of Molière in the Rue Richelieu, are things to be thankful for. The groups of statuary which make every garden valuable, the arches, monuments, and buildings erected to commemorate great deeds or fill important needs, are all as rich in loveliness as in usefulness. It is a question whether a republic could ever plan and perfect a city on such a scale of magnificence. The pressure of private interests, the impossibility of moving masses of people toward the same conception, is almost an insurmountable barrier to actions which are not based upon some necessity of business, education, material or public progress. The finer and more subtle advance which belongs to beauty in architecture, in sculpture, in painting, is apt to be lost sight of in more pressing needs; and the handling of the enormous sums of money requisite for such outlay is placed beyond the power of the people. But the only republics we know are too young yet to settle such doubts.

Let us leave the morning for the evening. If Paris shines in the daylight, it is absolutely phosphorescent in the darkness. Or is there any darkness? Myriads and myriads of electric lights; arches and groups and clusters of gas-jets in every conceivable nook and corner; many of the shops illuminated, all the *cafés* blazing. If carriages crowd through the day, they simply swarm now. Even on the smooth pavements the flying hoofs make a muffled thunder. Singing and dancing pavilions are outlined in lamps among the tree-shadows; a countless multitude drifts backward and forward over square and street. Every carriage has two large bright lights in front, that flash like clouds of glow-worms through the twilight distances. The great oval dome of the Hippodrome shines like a moonstone against the dark sky; sounds of music and revelry everywhere break the customary night quiet; elegance and fashion whirl by on the way to ball and opera; the bareheaded servant girl walks with her sweetheart through flickering light and shadow. The little tables on the side-walk are thronged with guests making merry over such an infinitesimal glass of wine as would not make a grasshopper tipsy. Are there any homes, any firesides, any groups of children gathered about father and mother; or is the whole world gone mad, and surging in an airy frolic through these dazzling streets? One might almost think so.

CHAPTER V.

A FESTIVAL DAY IN PARIS.

PARIS has as many sides as a faceted diamond, and each is as polished. It is the paradise of the rich; it is the elysium of the poor; it is old; it is new; it is at once the apotheosis of industry and of idleness. In its most ordinary aspect it transcends the gala entourage of almost any other city on the globe. In its festival dress on Sundays and fetes it is wholly unapproachable. It is not alone that its architectural effect is so splendidly adapted to brilliancy of display; that its wonderful avenues radiate in lines of palaces from the stars about the great monuments from which they start; that its streets and fountains, and statues and public places, make such superb centres from which the long, beautiful perspectives stretch away to the gentle heights in the distance. This is much, but it is not all. The genius of the people seems to ally itself to seasons of excitement and rejoicing. When other races are glad, this is jubilant; when other people simply enjoy, these go wild with delight. And this frenzy seems to be shared by their surroundings. One would say the very houses caught the enthusiasm.

To-day, with the subtle magnetism of to-morrow's opening in the air, the city seems to have gone mad altogether. The fact that the Exposition has been planned to commemorate the centenary of the great revolutionary movement of 1789 seems to rouse these impressible natures to an almost savage power of emotion. They shout, they laugh, they shriek wild phrases with harsh, guttural voices; they dance to choruses that have more of passion than of music in them. There is a sort of breathless fervour in the air. One feels as if at any moment the crowds might become mobs; yet everything is done decently and in order. Wide as the magnificent avenues are, they are narrow for the surging masses. The Champs Elysées is packed with a quivering, excited multitude waiting—for what? There is nothing beyond. It is only that the remembrance of a hundred years ago revives again in the hearts of the descendants of the citizens and citizenesses who dragged Louis XVI. to the guillotine, and spat at Marie Antoinette as she walked in sombre and lonely majesty from her death sentence.

The city is a marvellous picture of colour. How little we know as yet of the art of decoration as compared with this people. But then, too, how little we have to decorate! These marvellous highways of palaces, each with its double, triple, quadruple avenues of trees carrying the eye down their long vistas, these great Places grouped around some central magnificence of bronze or marble, these wonderful façades with the glory of Greece or Rome, or the florid beauty of the Renaissance, gathered about frieze, column, and peristyle—how can they help but be more marvellous, more magnificent, more wonderful than ever. Staffs of blue, of white, of red, of gold, "high as the mast of some tall Admiral," line the streets, lifting their burden of pendants, of banners, of shields above the tree tops, connected by long garlands of smaller flags, wound about and draped with slender scarfs of vivid colour. Sheafs of standards glowing in every conceivable elegance of form and tint brighten the beautiful stone arches of the bridges, decorate the entablatures of the windows, droop from the balconies, outline the eaves, the gables, the architectural lines. Forests of flags rise above the roofs, float from the boughs of the trees, wave even above the chimney tops. Every nation on the face of the earth is represented by its national emblems, but the tricolours outnumber them ten to one, and the effect is beyond expression. Small bands of soldiers march with swinging step hither and thither, detailed for duty to-night and to-morrow; soldiers in the long redingote of the Guard, the braided jacket of the Hussar, the blouse of the Zouave, the frogged coat of the Cuirassier. Here is the long horsehair plume, borrowed from the Uhlan, there the Prussian helmet, now the small French cap, then the fierce military shako. Officers with jingling swords and spurs, men with sabre and musket, uniforms of blue, grey, white, scarlet, they make a bouquet of brightness even among the people in their gaiety of Sunday clothes. Gas jets and ropes of globes are strung in every direction. They droop from the topmost pinnacles of the tallest buildings, falling to the ground in what will be long draperies of light; they hang like blossoms from the trees, they spring like flowers from the parterres of the parks and gardens. The great towers of the Trocadero, the domes of halls, the spires of churches are ready to blaze out in a galaxy of splendour so soon as night gives the necessary background. Surely never before, even in the palmy days of the Empire, was such a glory of brilliancy as this about to be lavished on the festival of the working people.

In the Place de la Concorde, as might be imagined, all this scintillance of form and colour centres. At each side of the Luxor obelisk, two staffs, nearly as tall as the monument itself, hold up silken scarfs of the most brilliant colour, with long pendants which twine about like fiery serpents. A perfect maze of gas jets, each bearing a globe of white light, winds in, out, and about in every conceivable direction. They cover the entire surface with an arabesque that soon will blaze with transcendent brilliancy. There is not a point of vantage left untouched. Even without illumination the effect is dazzling. It is hard to imagine what it may be with it. And between such an efflorescence of gilding, of silver, of scarlet, of purple in the swarm of floating banners, the sight grows dizzy.

Every park, square, and garden is radiant with life. Until late in the day there is an enormous proportion of children among the group. Such winsome darlings. There are adorable baby faces resting on the shoulders of stout Norman or Breton bonnes, their floating long robes almost sweeping the ground; there are pretty little dolls in white from tip to toe, all lace and silk; there are sturdy small boys with the invariable short stocking, showing bare, mottled legs from boot to knee, and the queer trousers wrinkled above; there are little girls in the simplest dresses that ever were formed for childhood, and other little girls in the most elaborate costumes that the fertile brain of a French modiste can conceive. The nurses are as picturesque as their charges, with their frilled white caps surmounted by a great turban of wide ribbon, from which two enormous floating ends reach within an inch or two of the dress hem. I wonder some daring soul has not introduced this innovation in America. What is the use of importing a French bonne shorn of her glory of peasant cloak and silken turban! What a sensation Madame would make in the Public Garden or Lincoln Park with one of these resplendent creatures occupying the front seat of the carriage with the latest hope of the house in her brawny arms!

One continuous stream of people has been passing since morning toward the Trocadero. This beautiful structure, erected for the purpose of containing the works of art during the Exposition of 1878, is to be one of the principal entrances to the present exhibition. It gives by far the most impressive view of the grounds and architectural plan of the buildings to be found in Paris. In one of its great square towers a huge elevator carries eighty persons at a time to an elevation of 220 feet. From the upper gallery thus reached, a most enchanting panorama presents itself. The natural rise of the ground from the level of the river banks added to the height of the tower gives a rise of over 300 feet, from which the eye seizes the entire plan of Paris within its semicircle of hills. The Seine, which makes a bold curve just at this point, stretches right and left under the lovely arches of the frequent bridges; the great avenues radiate from their different central stars; the lines of trees and palaces cross each other in a bewildering labyrinth of splendour, while the massive fronts of the great public buildings make each new point upon which the eye rests memorable. The towers of Notre Dame, the decorated dome of the Invalides, the ornate spire of St. Augustine, the fine lines of the Chamber of Deputies, especially claim attention. Facing the river the new Exposition Buildings fill the entire 120 acres of the surface of the Champ de Mars, and reach along the esplanades of the river as far as the bridge of Solferino far down its banks. In the immediate foreground are the beautiful Trocadero Gardens, with their green terraces descending to the bridge of Jena, their paths winding amid pavilions and fountains, with several of the smaller buildings connected with the Exposition among them. To-day all this portion is planted with lights and banners. The gardens look as if they had been sown with white lilies, so thick are the globes of gas jets; the enormous arcades stretching at each side of the central pavilion are crowded with pyramids of yellow lanterns placed between each of the close pillars; domes and towers are outlined in ropes of stars, and carry the same great pyramids like clusters of golden fruit high into the air. The winged statue of Fame which tops the central rotunda has been newly gilded, and shines, a dazzling image, in the sunlight. Across the water rise the main halls of the great exhibition. A wilderness of pagodas and minarets of every possible shape and description, fragile and massive, surround the principal buildings, which stretch their arched glass roofs on three sides of an enormous quadrangle. The middle space is a fairy garden of flowers, palms, fountains, and statues. But all about it what diverse and fantastic shapes! Domes tiled in blue and white, in deep sapphire and amber, in crystal, in bronze, in silver, in gold. Slender spires touched with carmine, glowing like malachite, armoured in shining scales, all tipped with flying streamers and floating banners, and airy figures with outstretched golden pinions, as if ready to fly to the ends of the earth to proclaim the glory of which they form part. Resplendent as the rest of the city is in its festival dress, this brilliant spectacle makes all the rest tame and quiet. One's eyes, weary with the brightness, turn for relief to the grey roofs and the tree embraced lines, the heights of Montmartre and the soft shadows of Père la Chaise.

Meantime, out at Versailles cannon are thundering, and the President of the Republic is being welcomed by shouts from thousands of loyal and lusty throats as he drives to open the ceremonial of the exhibition. Around him are grouped the great ones of the nation. There are Legrand and Christophle, with faces as English as any Londoner in the Strand; Lockroy, who would pass for an American save for his remarkable collar and loose necktie; Berger and Alphant, who represent wholly cosmopolitan types; and Tirard and Rouvier, French *du sang pur*. Not so pure, however, as Carnot himself, who has a strange resemblance to Gericke, but who is Gallic to his finger tips. In the midst of the desert of Sahara one would recognise him as a product of the Parisian boulevards. The national troops are drawn up before the gates of the chateau; the great orchestra is discoursing the strains of Berlioz's Marseillaise in the park gardens, and the "Great Waters" are beginning to flow through the magical system of fountains, from their rise in the Salle de Bal to the Baths of Diana and the grand basin of the Dragon. Truly, a wonderful and unforgetable sight. But prudent people, who value life and limb, will remain at home to read the account in to-morrow's journals instead of inviting destruction by trying to pierce through the surging crowds, who, on this anniversary of the revolution, may seethe into something of the old fury of '93 or the later madness of '71. At the best, a mass of people, with the reins of conduct held loose, and the ordinary rules of decorum lost in the license of excitement, is a dangerous entity. But a French mob, however good-natured, with the volatile disposition and mercurial temperament which belongs to it, is more dangerous than any. One could as soon depend upon the stability of quicksilver.

It is evening now, and the entire horizon is aglow with illuminations. There is not to be the general lighting up which is reserved for to-morrow night, but it is a sort of rehearsal. The great electric ball on the topmost point of the Eiffel Tower glows from its thousand feet of height like some new planet, more brilliant and scarcely smaller than the full moon, or like some enormous comet, drawn from its hiding place in heaven, and trailing its streamers of light across the dark sky. Now and again, from a point just beneath it, a smaller but equally bright ray shoots in this or that direction as it is turned upon its revolving basis, lighting up the farthest suburbs of Paris. From the Trocadero another enormous revolving wheel sends electric spokes of light swiftly flying over the city. Viewed from any of the bridges over the river this has the most weird effect. A great fan-shaped segment of white flame darts across the dark heavens, dazzlingly radiant at the base, and paling to the faintest glow of summer lightning at the summit, which broadens until it covers all the visible firmament. For an instant domes, spires, gables, and towers are touched into being out of the solemn shadow, to fade again as swiftly, until the next flash re-illumines; and this goes on indefinitely—a great star of radiance shooting its rays into eternity. It gives one a ghostly sensation to watch it noiselessly whirling through space. Every boat upon the Seine is glowing with Chinese lanterns and casting long reflections of coloured fire over the dark waters, which shine like black diamonds. The whole immense mass of the Chamber of Deputies is outlined in a double row of great lamps against the dense blackness of the starless night; the spire of St. Augustine lifts a pagoda-like cluster of golden balls above the house-tops. Darting rockets soar from the distant heights; flushes of ruby, of sapphire, of emerald, flame up and vanish. And between it all, laughing, singing, shouting, go the people, swaying from side to side of the broad streets, gathered on squares and bridges, sitting on the parapets of the river, crowding omnibuses and tramways, dashing about in the rapid small fiacres, anywhere, everywhere at once. For is it not Paris, and is this not the beginning of their own Festival? *A bas le chagrin! Vive la joie! Vive la France!*

CHAPTER VI.

THE GREAT EXPOSITION.

WHEN the Great Exposition of 1889 is a thing of the past it will have left much behind it beside the impress of its passing splendour. But even for this alone it might count as one of the landmarks of history. The marvellous beauty of arrangement about the grounds; the size and magnificence of the main buildings; the endless display of ingenuity and artistic taste manifested in the smallest details of decoration and construction, make up a scene of enchantment. The reproductions of human dwellings, from historic models of habitations fifteen or twenty centuries before Christ to those of every strange and far away nation of the present day, make one phase of boundless interest. Malay huts, built on piles in the midst of ponds, chalets of Switzerland and Norway, tents of Arabs, Mexican adobes, Tartar camps, Kaffir kraals, Indian wigwams, Russian isbas, Esquimaux snow huts, Bedouin encampments—there is no end to the variety. Even to dwellings of the Cave-men it is complete in its summary of history. Some of the Greek, Roman, Babylonian, and Assyrian houses are furnished with great delicacy both within and without, surrounded by the vegetation peculiar to their respective climates. Lanes and alleys shaded by trees and bright with flowers lead in every direction through this section, as carefully laid out as if they were destined to remain for ever.

The wonderful structure of Eiffel which dominates the

entire panorama, and which has created as great confusion of sentiment as its antitype the Tower of Babel did of tongues, is really not the grotesque monster its enemies would have one believe. Its extreme height gives an appearance of fragility which masks its strength, until one stands under the glorious sweep of the lower arches, springing from four fortress-like corners, and capable of enclosing an army. One feels a thrill of mystery, almost of awe, in looking up at the slender dark head lifted a thousand feet into the sky by day and the stars at night; and when red flames begin to burn about it, and the great electric light atop sends broad waves of white radiance across the darkness, it is almost supernatural. Mountains may climb to the skies, and giant precipices lift their frowning brows to heaven, but how should man dare aspire to such loftiness.

In the centre of the long pavilions devoted to the vineyards of France, the glass roofs of which are decorated in trellis work with twining leaves and tendrils painted with extreme delicacy around it, is the tun of wine sent by the vintners of Auvergnat. It contains 200,000 bottles of champagne; and the hogshead, which is as large as a house of two stories, twenty feet square, is ornamented with allegoric figures sitting amid vines and grapes. The French papers tell many amusing stories of the slow triumphal march of this monarch of casks to the capital. They pretend that hedges were torn down, streets widened, sides of houses and overhanging eaves torn away; and that one irate peasant, enraged at the indignity shown his dwelling, laid a spiritual habeas corpus upon the monster, and succeeded in holding it until damages had been paid him. The roadway between these pavilions is lined with growing specimens of vines from every wine-growing district in France, with small tablets recording the average productive power of each variety, with the cost and quality of the manufactured product. This, with the section at one end devoted to what might be called the pathology of the grape, including every form of morbid growth and insect which could impair its health and vigour, —must be of vast benefit to all interested in vine culture.

It is strange to note the intense sympathy of the people when sight or sound of military manœuvre reaches them. Something like a deep groan of content ran through the city like an electric shock at each boom of the cannon yesterday. When in addition the glare of bombs and fireworks lit up the sky in the evening, they too exploded with enthusiasm. Well-dressed men shouted with delight; bands of students and grisettes broke into the chorus of the Marseillaise or blew through penny trumpets. "*Mais, c'est magnifique,*" said a stalwart young workman near us, as boom and flash came together: "*C'est presque comme une émeute!*" As if a riot or a revolution were the dearest thing on earth. Alas, have they not yet learned the danger of playing with edge tools? When they remember so bitterly, how can they forget so easily.

How little the Queen of Sheba would have thought of the glory of Solomon if she could have walked through the Central Pavilion to-day. Inside the great dome, with its wealth of glass golden stained, and its wonderful symphony of colour from amber to orange, the light falls in a rain of mellow sunshine, rich but not glaring, which might have heralded the descent of Jove to Danae. The superb dimensions are so well balanced that one gets no impression of the actual size until figures help the understanding. The fine frieze representing in triumphal procession all the nations of the earth, is set like a band of rare tapestry in the gold of the decorated wall, half way up the three hundred feet of height. It is a splendid study of the value of yellow. Beyond stretch the blue and grey arches of the main pavilion, with the main tint so overlaid with arabesques in soft warm hues that one can scarce detect the original background; and under the great arcades, radiant with frescoes and gilding, whatever has been accomplished for the prosperity, the helpfulness, the luxury of humanity, is gathered in masses. Here are potteries and ceramics from every great house in the world which has won fame in this direction. Here is the jewelled glass of Bohemia and Hungary, like constellations of brilliants held in shape by a mesh of golden sunbeams, or silver moonlight, glittering, flashing, scintillant with precious stones, as full of fire as their brethren of the mine. Here are the gems themselves woven into parure and necklace, fashioned into ear and finger jewels; in bracelets and brooches and zones, in stars and sprays and delicate frost work, as evanescent as the rays which break from them. And wealth of beaten gold and silver; and tapestries more beautiful than those the queens of old worked for royal banqueting halls; and carpets which would muffle the tread of an army; and rugs from Turkey and Persia, with the strange dark beauty of the fabled dyes of Tyre glowing in their barbaric richness. Here are couches so carved that they seem to belong more to Eastern seraglios than to western civilisation; perfumes as delicate and subtle as those of dreams; bronzes full of untamed strength and wild motion; Italian marbles like frozen snow images; velvets and satins for the robes and mantles of empresses; robes and mantles themselves, draped into such folds of grace as never were known in the history of dress. And with these, every device known to human ingenuity for lightening of labour and saving of time; helps for work and for play, for high and lowly, for home and abroad, for sickness and health; helps innumerable for keeping alive that blessed peace of which this whole festival is but a token. No wonder the heart swells in beholding, for this is the holiday of labour, the crowning triumph of industry. It is not the might of kings which has brought about these marvels, but the honest toil and ceaseless industry of the common people. These and these alone have offered the golden key which opens these doors of fairyland.

But after all, it is the Pavilion of Liberal Arts which marks the highest point of hopefulness and progress here, as in the real work of the world. Material treasures, rare and precious as they are, appeal only to the senses, and they seduce rather than uplift. To produce them, it is still labour of hands, strength of muscle, sweat of the brow which is necessary. Of themselves, they do not greatly change the condition of the peoples who produce them. Apotheosis of industry though this be, there are yet woes and injustices inherent in the very causes which command its production. Slaves of the lamp and the mine still toil and serve under the worst conditions of bondage, in order that these glories shall flash before the unaccustomed eyes of men. The lacemaker, losing eyesight over her pillow; the little children chained to the mill wheels of Manchester and Birmingham; the Indian weaver spending weary years over one product of his loom, barely sustained by the scant wage it affords him—these too are commemorated in this glowing pile of riches. But the guiding touch, the elevating thought which wins them little by little from degradation, which replaces the curse of labour by its blessing, which carries light and recompense and well-earned rest to the homes and bodies of the toilers, these spring from the enlightenments Education brings; and the tools with which she works are in that plain pavilion yonder. The living principle, the *motif* of this grand Festival Overture is there, a thousandfold more than in any of its more brilliant variations. It is the chemistry and electricity, it is the silent struggle of science with the forces of matter, which have made it possible to uplift those shining banners of victory. And in these directions it is good for an

American to see how far Edison has distanced all his fellow-workers. It is a splendid showing, for everything here adds to the firm fibre of the soul, and lifts the mortal into relation with the Infinite. Every instrument which the genius of man has dedicated to the higher uses of science is here, with the name which has made it famous. No country and no race has been forgotten, and the roll of honour stretches from end to end of the vast building.

Next to this probably in value, because of the power they wield as an artistic impulse and an education to the spiritual element in man, are the exhibits of painting and sculpture. Naturally those of France both in number and excellence lead the rest; though England represents a brilliant galaxy of names in its smaller collection, and the United States has a very creditable display. When it is remembered that France alone sends 1447 canvases, most of them large, and many of heroic size; 228 pastels and water-colours; 138 architectural designs; 455 etchings; and 568 pieces of sculpture and engraving on medals, the scope occupied in their exhibition may be imagined. Great Britain has five or six large halls with specimens from most of her best modern names, and a large number of works already made known to us by engravings. "Cherry Ripe," "Bubbles," "At Evening Time there shall be Light," and "The Return of the Fishing-Boat," were some of these. Austria-Hungary had nearly as many; among them Munkacsy's "Christ before Pilate," and "Crucifixion," with the usual number of scoffers and admirers regarding both. Spain has a veritable chamber of horrors; nearly all the large pictures having for subjects most brutal and bloody scenes, magnificently executed, so that it is quite a physical effort to overcome the repulsion they produce. Russia has the merit of having chosen individual types and events from among its own people. Too many of the other nations are satisfied with following French models and subjects, so that they lose character and atmosphere. Out of the haze of general impressions which one carries away from this department a few canvases stand out vividly, like the wonderful portraits of Carolus Duran, the illusive, haunting figure of one of Whistler's beauties, or Detaille's band of mounted soldiers, singing as they wind along a curving path through the marshes. The dash and ease of motion are remarkable in this. A warm sunset glow is in the sky behind, with the light reflected in shallow pools along the way; the pale sickle of the new moon shines faintly above; one of the leaders clashes a pair of cymbals, another shakes a tambourine, while a third, turning in his saddle, beats time for the comrades behind. One can fancy the Marseillaise rolling into the soft evening air with accompaniment of jingling spur and muffled tramp of horses, while a white haze of dust rises about the knees of the men. Among the portraits there is the unmistakable stamp of the Parisienne. The clear paleness of tint, the large spirituelle eyes, the veiled touch of *espièglerie*—too fine for roguishness and too demure for coquetry, but still a combination of both—and the innate grace of pose, make the pictured forms quite unlike any other race of women. There is a much smaller proportion of the nude than we have been accustomed to see in French Exhibitions at home; and less too of that sentimental sickly green in the landscapes which looks as if nature had been washed out.

The Hall of Sculpture is rich throughout its endless length with beauty. But the nude figures are more aggressive; the Dianas, of which there must be a dozen, have a flavour of the demi-monde which scarce suits the goddess of chastity. The Greek purity which so permeated form as to make it divine and passionless has not yet been found by modern sculptors, at least when French blood is in their veins. But there are many beautiful and stately conceptions: a tender youthful Antigone leading the blind Oedipus; heroic forms, struggling or victorious; vestal virgins; mothers with laughing babes in arm; a gracious figure of Pestalozzi with children looking lovingly into the kind face; a youth with fine fury in his desperate glance holding the head of a dying comrade, while he speeds his last arrow at the foe. Imagine hundreds and hundreds of these and kindred subjects, standing in white silence in a stately hall lighted throughout by a glass roof supported on slender blue pillars, with walls panelled in dull red and hung with antique drapery, and you get some idea of this division of the Pavilion of Fine Arts at the Great Exposition.

CHAPTER VII.

THE VICTORIES OF PEACE AND LABOUR.

THE French journals overflow, with great reason, in felicitations on the success of the Exposition. They congratulate the people upon the fact that this great centralisation of interests marks the entrance of France again to its old position as mistress of the world in the specialties she had made her own. *Figaro* quotes Heine's apostrophe to his beloved Paris : " O my beautiful Lutice ! You shall not be replaced in your sovereign power by that other capital which is but the white Timbuctoo of Europe, as Timbuctoo is the black Berlin of Africa." When one reads the enthusiastic comments of the Press in other countries, one is not surprised at such outbursts. This enterprise was frowned down by mostly every government, on the ground of its association with revolutionary principles, yet its consummation has forced the most unstinted commendation from Vienna, Pesth, St. Petersburg, Italy, Belgium, England, America, and even Prussia itself.

If the other divisions of this World's Fair deserve the names of Temples of Industry, consecrated to the religion of peace and labour, the pavilion devoted to machinery might be called its Cathedral. The span of the glass and iron arch is so immensely broad and high, and the quarter of a mile length so tremendous, that it gives the effect of stepping into the open air after the closeness and draperies of the other portions. It is always thronged ; for though few comprehend the principles of machinery, there are fewer who are not interested in its manifestations. On every side of this great expanse, stationary and movable bridges rise in the air; every form and variety of motive force has its special representation; the inventive genius of the age finds its highest expression. An army of workmen attend the movements of these wonderful constructions—mind serving matter. Another army hidden from sight under foot feeds the fires and regulates the batteries which form the vital principle of this world of motion. What an idea of the concentration produced by association it gives to see the dependence of each part on the other. What an argument for freedom in the interchange of thought and action among men!

America—outside Edison—seems to be losing her old prestige in invention. The American temperament, eager, curious, morbidly active, has always appeared particularly fitted for the evolution of ways and means, especially in material forms. But up to this time little has been done in the training of nature beyond sharpening this blind instinct on the whetstone of emulation and greed of gain. Meantime the older and wiser nations have gone on patiently teaching, carefully preparing, laying the foundation for clear understanding and exact execution; and they are beginning to beat us on our own ground. The audacity which leads us to be first in experiment is very well, but it should be supplemented by better things. For many years now the eyes of political economists and educators among us have been open to the evils arising from decay of the apprentice system and delay in founding industrial schools. Our tradespeople are becoming more and more machine-tenders, knowing little and caring less about anything beyond the crank they turn, or the atom of wood or iron they place in a slot. There is no motive for thought, and scarce any need of judgment. An intelligent monkey could be taught to do the same thing.

So when we need brains as well as manipulation we are forced to import Belgian or French trained artisans.

In trying to sum up the results of the Exposition, there is one issue, not readily recognised by the general public, which will probably be found in the future to have given as great an impetus to the cause of human progress as all the rest of this great, magnificent, tangible creation which it supplements. This is, the series of international congresses to be held in Paris during the months covered by the Exhibition. Through June, July, August, September, and October, seventy of these reunions have been arranged, embracing delegates from all lands, and lasting each from five to ten days. There is scarce a phase connected with the higher civilisation of mankind which is not recognised in this splendid programme. Every form of legal and medical jurisprudence; the rights of labour and employers; questions of philanthropy, industry, and sanitation; education in all its branches; inventions; the discussion of peace; industrial schools: physical training; women's needs and aspirations; temperance—all the topics which bear upon the welfare of the individual and the political economy of nations, have each their time and place for study and discussion. The names which head the different commissions as presidents include many of the most distinguished in France. Jules Simon in literature, Levasseur in education, Mascart in electricity, Meissonier in art, Eiffel in engineering, Fabret, Brouardel, and Charcot in medicine, Leon Say, Passy, Janssen, and David each in their specialties, speak sufficiently for the interest these advanced minds take in the subjects endeared to them by thought and study. It is among the army of specialists which these men lead, and in the ranks of this Legion of Honour, that the motto chosen for this universal festival, "Pax et Labor," finds meaning and strength. A century ago peace would have been as sounding brass or tinkling cymbal amid the forces of the world. It is to the persistent effort, the quiet but ceaseless agitation, the inculcation of purer and nobler principle which this group represents, that we owe whatever has been gained in making right, rather than might, arbiter in the affairs of men. The richer the hostages given to fortune in this regard, the stronger the foundations upon which the prosperity of society rests, the more difficult it becomes to move the mind to a belief in the necessity for strife; and what Christianity has been painfully and slowly accomplishing for nearly two thousand years, the increased intelligence of the majorities which make public opinion will produce in a hundred. The magnificent step taken by England and America in settling their Alabama claims by arbitration is being followed slowly but surely toward the platform of universal peace. And this Exposition of 1889 is one of the broad lifts upward, since it signalises the triumph of the people in the quiet paths of order and industry, rather than the prestige of rulers and the false glory of brute force.

As if to vindicate themselves from any suspicion of dependence upon the will of their respective governments, and to prove how thoroughly they have learned to live in and for themselves, the people have flooded these two or three hundred acres of space with an inconceivable marvel of wealth. It is like flinging the velvet glove which covers the iron hand of labour in the face of power. Walking through the endless aisles, dazzled by the infinite variations of refinement and luxury everywhere, one could not help repeating the legend which Revelation offered to Faith, and applying to this temporal kingdom a phrase meant only for the heavenly. Truly "it hath not entered into the heart of man to conceive" the glories of this world which man hath created. It is a little interesting to note that France, in the miles of avenues along which her products are exhibited, is surpassed by the other nations competing in many specialties which used to be considered exclusively her own. There is nothing in her jewellery so original and exquisite as the designs of Tiffany of New York or Christessen of Copenhagen. Her glass is dull beside the jewelled splendours of Bohemia; her lace less delicate than the hoar-frost daintiness of Belgian handiwork; her watches commonplace when compared with those of Swiss manufacture. Even in fashion, Redfern of London has the most artistic costumes as well as the richest. But her Limoges faience is superb, and the Sevres as miraculous of tint and tender in decoration as ever; her tapestries as marvellous as the paintings of the old masters they reproduced; and in the countless little prettinesses upon which so much of the pleasure of ordinary life depends she is still supreme.

It is rather remarkable to note, through the different departments of the main exhibition of industrial arts, the prevalence of a return to old forms and designs, instead of an attempt to push original conceptions. In the patterns of laces, the colours and effects in draperies, the forms of iron, wood, and metals, this is most noticeable. The Hungarian potteries and Bohemian glass show it in a very marked degree. One can trace the effect of the Cypress collections which have been made familiar to designers by Cesnola; and the discoveries of Haussmann have certainly had a strong bearing upon recent workmanship. It gives a grace and beauty to outward shape that is extremely grateful to the eye, and a harmony both of tint and ornamentation to which we have often been unused. Some of the Danish jewellery is particularly good in this respect. The gold brooches, whether enamelled or in the natural colour, are very beautiful—above all some crosses dating from the time of Canute and the early centuries. The bucklers and shields of the Norse heroes are strongly suggested by these richly ornamented creations, which have an artistic value wholly beyond their intrinsic worth. They are as rare and fine in their simpler way as the wonderful jewelled orchids of Tiffany in their extreme splendour. Nothing so gorgeous as these last, in jewels, has ever been offered before, and they are as amazing for originality as for beauty. They are one of the triumphs of modern artistic training.

The Italian lamps are another compliment to the past, in the ancient forms which have been so closely copied. These are wondrously elegant and decorative, whether in wrought black iron or costlier silver. Compared with the tawdry effects of the usual manufactured articles they are pure works of art. But to one who sees for the first time France, Italy, or any of these earlier nations, it is not strange that in such productions their work should so outrank our own. The whole life of their people is passed among the purest artistic influences. The houses they live in, the churches and cathedrals which play so large a part in their education, the façades of their public buildings, the fountains, arches, monuments, statues, terraces—each and everything is a training of the senses and the imagination. Already to start from, they are at a point which we can only reach by great effort in centuries. It is impossible not to be impregnated with the spirit of refinement and grace which is so omnipresent; and when to this is added the more impressionable and plastic nature, there can be but one result. Each has its specialties in which it is most successful, as each has the fauna and flora which belong to its climatic conditions; but always art, which is but an emigrant with us, is indigenous here. Pray heaven that we may ever reach the time when we too may hail it as a gift of nature rather than of grace!

The shopkeepers and theatre managers complain that the attractions of the Exposition Grounds in the evening draw their customers away, and leave the streets empty. Who wonders that they succumb to the enchanting beauty of alleys and walks outlined in fire and blazing with light until they are positively unearthly. Every garden bed is full of strangely luminous flowers; the great domes shine against the sky in outlines of flame; the Eiffel Tower, with its lofty platforms illuminated, throws revolving shafts of lightning far into the dense blackness of the upper atmosphere. The encampments of restaurants, with their platoons of small tables laden with ices, cake, and wine, are resonant with a running fire of clattering spoons and clinking glasses; bands are playing in the stands here and there; the oriental quarters are tinkling with dancing feet and barbaric music; cascades of water are falling in showers of diamonds, emeralds, and topaz. It would be surprising if the long bright avenues outside were not emptied. But are they? The sky is reddened with the glare of the customary illumination; joyous strains from the concert halls are in the air; revellers of every grade and sex are on their way to public or private amusements; the concierge holds a reception of his friends at each courtyard gate; all is life, bustle, animation. Where could we pack that other quarter of a million if the Exposition gates should suddenly open? Do not be afraid. You would never be conscious of it. What are a few waves more or less to the swell of the ocean?

I believe the strongest charm of this city is its appearance of leisure. A sort of careless ease disguises every effort, as the smooth whiteness of the skin hides the knitting of the muscles. There is something grateful and relaxing to worried minds and bodies in this outward seeming of a world which takes life graciously, unhurriedly. It is then possible to be prosperous, happy, and undriven at the same time! It is possible to combine rational exertion which shall be sure to bring rational reward, with time to look about one, to smile in the face of a friend, to gambol with one's children, to be impelled by fancy or inclination, instead of being wound up like a machine. How soothing it is. So the tension unconsciously relaxes, and the balm of restfulness begins to work. There never was a place where, without moral qualm or struggle, one resigns himself to idleness as in Paris. There is so much to distract. The attention is carried so completely away from self to interest in the beautiful surroundings. History lives so in the streets and walls. Such a Walhalla of spirits opens before one, majestic, powerful, picturesque; forces that centuries ago moved the world into the paths it is now treading. And all in such a setting, such a golden framework of magnificence, as satisfies every desire of the heart. There is no emotion, no aspiration left unsatisfied; and the gratification is so subtle, it is transmitted through such a radiance of atmosphere, that one is conscious only of the result of satisfaction without any effort in attaining it.

CHAPTER VIII.

AMONG THE PARIS CHURCHES.

ALTHOUGH Notre Dame is considered by critics to be lacking in many essential architectural points, and to lose much of its impressiveness from the changed character of its surroundings, it moves the stranger who regards it from without or within with a great force of reverence. The square through which it is approached gives the requisite perspective for the singular beauty of its façade, rising like an immense reredos in a lofty screen of sculptured stone, surmounted by the pierced arches of its upper gallery. The delicate carvings of the square towers, and the mass of figures, medallions and allegorical subjects, which encrust the three great portals, lend richness to the dark grey granite that might otherwise be too sombre. To the very tips of the parapets, this beautiful confusion of traceries, bas-reliefs, and statues continues; the diabolic and grotesque in the shape of monsters and animals, being mingled with the devotional in gargoyle and fretted work, in an infinite variety of detail. Not an inch of space is left unimproved, as if loving labour sought to lavish its best care and thoughtfulness upon the decoration. Viewed from the side, the effect is equally fine, with the strange, slender, arrow-shaped spire rising from the centre of the long roof line, and the airiness of flying buttresses lightening the majestic height of the wall. But it is the interior which most greatly seizes the imagination. The profound depth and height, full of sombre dimness, through which the faint light from the stained glass of the high choir windows at the upper end falls brokenly; the massive pillars rising from the obscurity of dark aisles and flowering into the climbing arches of the roof; the occasional radiance of the rich glass in the side chapels, half hiding, half revealing, the groups of white marble statues and monuments which they contain; and the enormous effect of distance which the extreme height and narrowness of the central nave produces, is grandly impressive. Here and there, noiseless figures appear for a moment and vanish again; a breath of fragrance and the glimmer of waxen tapers, mark some shrine of the Virgin or the saints, which is a special focus of devotion. If it is Sunday, the candles of the High Altar draw faint points of radiance from the gold and white robes of the officiating priests, and the voices of the choir break in distant echoes among the arches, with the shrill, sweet treble of the boys, like a tangle of bird notes rising high above. There is a smell of incense in the air, a pale odour of sanctity. As the eye grows more accustomed to the gloom, faint silhouettes of figures in the dark soutanes of priests, or purple cope of a bishop, relieve themselves from the deep, carved chairs surrounding the sanctuary, as they murmur responses to the prayers. The voice of the celebrant is wholly lost in the distance, or comes only like a sigh of wind through pine-trees. The congregation, kneeling where the light falls most strongly, is yet in a chiaroscuro full of Rembrandt's dearest effects. A sense of awe takes possession of one. Could one ever reach the end of those mystic aisles? Are those men, or the shadows of men, moving beyond? From the darkness of those sombre arches are not the intrigue and the glory of past ages still ready to seize upon one in all its horror and enchantment? Is it the sixteenth or the nineteenth century which is ruling the world? No place I have ever entered, even those wonderful carved galleries of the Louvre, filled with memories of Catherine de Medicis and the royal ghosts of history, haunted by the more than regal power of Mazarin and Richelieu, animated by the stately and fateful presence of Marie Antoinette, with the bright head of her hapless darling by her side—has held the fascination of tradition so strongly about it as this grave and solemn cathedral. For has not this too borne witness before all that silent host? Have not their arrogance and pride flashed in passing splendour through these dark arches also; and, let us hope, some moments of humility and earnestness lifted their prayers to God? That strange, pompous, unnatural life could not have been wholly without divine instincts, strained though it was through so many subtleties. And saints as well as sinners have consecrated these altars; the world's heroes, as well as its sycophants, have moved over these worn pavements. Why should not the higher influence be the strongest.

None of the other churches exercise quite the same fascination. The Madeleine with its severe Greek elegance of outline, and its niched cordon of saintly figures to preserve it from the profanation of the outer world, is too modern to move the fancy greatly. An edifice begun only in the middle of the last century, and completed in the early portion of this, which would be respectable antiquity with us, is but a babe in long clothes among these elder representatives of the religious family. But it is still, as all babes should be, beautiful and interesting. The management of the light, which falls wholly from circular windows in the vaulted roof, is very effective. So are the marks of the bullets here and there in the walls; reminiscences of the three hundred communists shot within their shelter by the national troops during the outbreak following the Franco-Prussian war. The groups of statuary within the church are really fine: and the congregations represent the wealth and fashion of Paris. The preachers connected with the parish would seem also to be the most eloquent and brilliant, for the sermons are always delivered with magnificent rhetorical effect. It is pretty to see the great flight of stone steps leading to the main entrance covered with children after their first communion; the girls dressed like little brides, covered from head to foot with transparent veils, and shining in their snowy robes like a flock of white doves; the boys like jack-daws with white waistcoats, and trousers, and black jackets. The sweet serious faces, and the sense of mingled devotion and importance in their manner, are charming, as they trip away surrounded by every available member of their family as a guard of honour. The Madeleine seems to be especially chosen for all ceremonies. It is scarcely possible that the ordinary happenings of its own parish could provide such a series of marriages and funerals as are daily to be seen issuing from its portals. It is difficult to say which, as spectacles, are most imposing, the wedding processions, with white favours on the horses' heads and harness, white satin curtains and linings in the carriages, bouquets in the grooms' button-holes, and the dazzling figure of the Nouvelle Mariée as she moves among her bevy of attendant nymphs; or the lugubrious trappings of the woeful vehicles, with mournful draperies of densest black shrouding even the poor quadrupeds, with their numberless major-domos in cocked hats and black staffs of office, and drivers in broad sashes and shining Wellington boots reaching nearly to the waist. Then such marshalling of flowers, such wreaths of tinsel and beads, such broad cloth-dressed mourning coaches, such

> "Windy suspirations of forced breath,
> And the dejected 'havior of the visage,"

make really an affecting spectacle for the senses, if not

for the heart. I am not sure but that for theatrical properties the funeral excels all the other demonstration in effectiveness.

But no matter what church one enters, there is sure to be something to move the imagination which heretofore has been fed only on the prevalent stucco and gewgaw tawdriness of the new world. Under the dim arches one will come upon altars and pulpits by Viollet le Duc and his brothers in genius, if not in fame; windows as exquisite as the most delicate fancy and richest tints can make them; frescoes and pictures from the hands of artists who have long made their country famous; and groups of sculpture as rare in execution as in the events they commemorate. You may hear Gounod leading his Ave Maria at a vesper service, or Saint Saens presiding at the great organ through the mass. You will find great names that belong to history, whose relics repose under the flags you tread; and everywhere reminiscences of honourable men and celebrated deeds fill the mind with retrospection. It is not what meets the eyes alone, beautiful though that may be, which moves the spirit. It is the power of the past, stronger in such scenes than any force of the present which holds one captive. Simply to walk under the roof of a building which represents a thousand years of time, and which has looked upon the changing fortunes of kings and people from the days of Charlemagne to our own, is a sensation not to be despised or rejected.

It would be small wonder if this entire nation were one of artists. So much to rouse the imagination is in the stones about one; so many forms of grace and loveliness are there to lift out of the narrowness of commonplace association. But the more one sees of the lower classes in this city the less one is encouraged to look for such traits in them. There is a species of brutality, unconscious but real, in the faces of many of the poorer men which is very striking —a look of satisfaction with the lower pleasures of the moment, without a trace of sentiment or aspiration to soften the harshness of material life. It might be called an expression made up of animal instinct, if one should attempt to classify it; and their manners would belong to the same category. To women they are boorish, to strangers insolent, to horses cruel. This is all the more strange when contrasted with the easy and exquisite courtesy that is so prominent among the upper classes, or even with the vivacity and brightness of temperament among themselves. They look like people to whom even horror would bring delight, if the only alternative were calm and even action. We were struck one day with the unholy glee, the outburst of coarse humour with which one of the coachmen related to us some of the most terrible experiences during the commune, when questioned about places in passing. He described with strong pantomimic effect the murder of the Archbishop and thirty others inside the prison of La Roquette, laughing immoderately over the way in which the pools of blood stained the flags of the yards and spurted upon the walls. His grins and leers and little clucks with the tongue would have been fiendish if the feeling which produced them had not been so impersonal. He was simply telling a good story, and desired to make it as vivid as possible; but the human element of the case, its pathos and terror, affected him no more than if he were speaking of a struggle of insects on an ant-hill. At another time we had almost the same experience, in a description of the memorable struggles of the "Bloody week" of May 27, 1871, between the troops and Communists at Père la Chaise. "It was a fine time; firing here, firing there; thousands killed; all smoke and noise." One would have thought the remembrance, even eighteen years after, enough to soften the eyes and the voice of any one who had lived through those terrible days; but no, it was part of a drama, comedy or tragedy, who cared? Yesterday, when the Revolutionists celebrated the anniversary of this same week, marching with red banners draped in mourning and crowned with wreaths of flowers, the speeches and sentiments spoke neither of grief nor of glory. They were cries for more blood; ferocious enthusiasm for some future day when anarchy and confusion should be again rampant. As the ranks reformed after the demonstration, thunder began to growl from a dark cloud in the west. "Ha! citizen; doesn't that remind you of '71? It might be the mitrailleuses." "It is a good omen. Let us pray that we will soon hear it nearer; within our walls, rolling through our Boulevards." And I believe if this happened to-morrow many of the people would forget the dread and danger in their delight at the smell of gunpowder and the chance of a new sensation. If such recklessness sprang from some deep love of principle which prefers suffering to injustice it would be heroic; where it comes only from the restlessness that craves excitement it is unnatural.

Of all the world what a city is this to have been so often drunk with the intoxication of blood and fury! These broad, bright spaces which seem made for light and gladness; the brilliant Boulevards; the shining river winding in and out among palaces and gardens; the thousand forms of interest and amusement which crowd the busy streets! One's preferences are sorely tried. At times the New Paris, with its magnificent sweeping vistas, its wealth of fountains and flowers, the irresistible wave of luxury and beauty which draws the sensuousness of humanity whither it will, seems bravest and most beautiful. One would remain for ever in that region of loveliness about the Bois, the Arc de Triomphe, and those Elysian Fields which are lovelier than any in which the Deities of old ever lingered. But the scene changes and now it is that wonderful world of Old Paris which takes possession of the fancy. One stands by the river front of the Louvre, where every corridor and window frames the glory of the past, and looks across the grey arches of Pont Neuf towards the Isle de St. Louis and the towers of Notre Dame. The golden spires of La Sainte Chapelle are glowing in the warm June sunshine, every street and lane about is full of some reminiscence of past glory; even the names recall the old days when the magnificence of the Grand Monarque was the wonder of a dazzled world. The touch of the present adorns without changing it, as the bouquets of the flower-girl yonder cover the old wall of the embankment on which they rest. Every spire and gable about one is softened to the eye by the dust of centuries; and something deeper than even the most exquisite satisfaction of sense thrills heart and soul with its power. Is it not here after all that one is nearest the real heart of the city. Let us thank kind fortune that one can decide in favour of either, or of both.

CHAPTER IX.

THE PARISIAN AT HOME.

IT is not strange that the true Parisian loves his Paris, and pines for it even when fate carries him no farther away than the provinces of France. If more unkind circumstance buffets him against the shores of a land conservative as England, or immature as America, instead of the bright, responsive world upon which he has become dependent, small wonder that he turns from the allurements they offer with indifference. He has inherited by nature the temperament a certain brilliant Bostonian attained by grace; he can better do without the comforts of life than its luxuries. He can better accept the passing straits of simple deprivation than miss the glamour of those brilliant streets, that pomp and circumstance of external magnificence, that effervescent bubble of excitement which rises so continuously here to the brim of the cup of life. He misses being amused without effort, and having the stage scenery shifted constantly before him for the comedy of humanity. He misses the ease of movement which makes friction unobservable, and the grace of manner which makes society a delight. There may be greater fortune and brighter fame to be won in the distant land, but the effort to seize them is too heroic. Better stay poor in Paris than be rich elsewhere. If he cannot be in the swim, at least he can stand on the banks and watch. He can catch the scent of the flowers, he can hear the echoes of the music, he can count the flying figures as they dance. And he can feel himself part of it all. The great, glittering, beautiful city is his for delight; his to be fond of; his to be proud of. He does not want your heavy and costly dinner; the *petits plats* of the gay restaurant served under the trees in the open air suit his appetite and his purse. He does not appreciate the sad and tedious enjoyment of your pompous entertainments; here are the cafés, the theatres, the drive on the Boulevard or in the Bois, to be had for a song. "Vanity of vanities; there is nothing new under the sun" of the rest of the world. In Paris there is nothing old. It is for ever swept out of sight by some fresh wave of novelty. Why should he not be satisfied? And he is.

Not that the Parisian is obliged to do without comforts; far from it. A few of the mechanical contrivances on which we pride ourselves he does not know; and it is a question whether ignorance is not bliss with him. So many of our modern improvements are delusions and snares. They close some little chink of immediate discomfort and open a wide door through which permanent distress enters. Our systems of heating and our water-supply are both more ingenious and plentiful than those abroad; but when one reflects on the disadvantages of a kiln-dried atmosphere through six months of the year, and the fatal influence of sewer gas in our city houses, the gain is more apparent than real. Even in these respects, as well as in almost every other material advantage, the Frenchman outranks us. He has choice of two prices for his omnibus. He is never harassed by being forced to stand during transit, or torn limb from limb in trying to force egress or ingress through the compact crowd massed in the car. Each vehicle has its printed regulation number of places; each of these places is divided by a light rail from the next, and, to make assurance doubly sure, a commissionaire at each of the regular halting stations on the route sees practically that only the number required to fill the vacant spaces enters. There is no confusion, no pushing, and tearing, or growling, or swearing. The person who arrives earliest at the station receives a numbered slip, which gives him the first right to enter the coming omnibus; the next receives the second, and so on. It is first come first served, and the order is never broken. No doubt there is some annoyance when one is in a great hurry; but one is so rarely in a great hurry in this wise city. It is one of the evil factors eliminated from life. There is so much to absorb, to interest, to amuse; why should one allow the perverse imp of worry and haste to gain possession of his more reasonable faculties? So the tired man or woman is always sure that his omnibus trip at least will be rest and refreshment, especially if he has the courage of his convictions and mounts on top. For there by far the best panorama of the city streets is obtained. The average carriage is too low to allow any sweep of vision. The horse's head in front, or the passing fiacre at the side, hems one in as closely as a moving *cul de sac;* but the second story of a tramway or an omnibus is perfect. Unless one's vanity is particularly rampant there is no loss of dignity involved. Monsieur in the last degree of Parisian elegance, Madame in lace and velvet, occupy their places with perfect decorum. *He* can puff his cigarette without poisoning the lower air; *she* can trip up and down the comfortable winding staircase without showing more than a glimpse of ankle or embroidered skirt. (I am not quite sure but that a true Parisienne prefers this to showing no glimpse at all.) As for Mademoiselle, she is never seen inside or out, above or below, without mamma, papa, or the maid as a bodyguard.

He has—we are still following in the wake of our

Parisian—the comfort, summer and winter, of infinitely clean streets, which are a delight to the senses in every way. Each morning after the sweeping is done, water pipes are opened directly above the gutters and a full, flowing stream is turned on which washes every sign of impurity down through the openings leading to the upper system of sewers. A few dexterous sweeps of the long brooms help any lingering dirt to find its way into the channel prepared for it; and for some time after a rivulet of bright water ripples over the clean pavement with the pleasant tinkle of running brooks. It is the most æsthetic mode of street cleaning in existence. Then he has a total exemption from dust. Over the perfect roadways and wide cemented sidewalks there is exercised the most constant care. Watering-carts pass in the morning, and at all hours of the day the queer street hose, mounted like a centipede on small wheels at each joint, is used to keep the upper surface fresh without being muddy. It is not done once and for all; if necessity requires it twice, it is sprinkled twice; if ten times, it is sprinkled ten. There are always plenty of men in the city's service. The idea of the local government, at least, seems to be to employ as many, instead of as few, as possible in the State's service. We heard one day, as a reason given for not hiring typewriting machines in the municipal clerk's office, that a few men could then do the work which now required two hundred. This is in keeping with the paternal policy the republic maintains towards its sons, partly no doubt from a feeling of its efficacy in government, partly from pride. In things that concern the beauty of the city there is no stint in appropriations. Departments are not put off with a miserly proportion of their demands for working capital; and no fraudulent scheme of economy to further the future campaigning policy of the ruling powers is allowed to interfere with the order, the cleanliness, or the educational projects of town or country. Young as the French republic is, it has already learned some lessons that older pupils in the same school find it difficult to commit to memory. Then he has about him that alert, brilliant vivacity that seems to belong to the very air of the city, and be as much a characteristic of its people as any other mental or physical trait. The glancing eye, the speaking gesture, the flashing smile, the responsive temperament, the swiftness of comprehension, that appears to give and receive impressions by a look or a motion, make a by-play full of sensation and novelty, upon which he unconsciously depends for entertainment. He may be no more—he may even be less deeply interested in the actual occupation which makes his life; but how full of sensation and novelty is the routine of existence! What a scintillant and electric intelligence takes the place of the heavy, slow comprehension which prevails in other localities! And where else but in Paris can he make good its loss?

The habits of life, so far as regards eating, are better with our Parisian. England and America both transgress, one in the quantity, the other in the quality, of food. The Briton feeds too heavily. He becomes plethoric and beefy. The exquisite rose-tints on his daughter's cheek turn to patches of harsh colour on the face of his wife; and his own rubicund visage suggests chronic congestion. Not content with heavy meals morning, noon, and evening, there is a night supper, more or less profuse according as the good sense of the individual bends to or wrestles with custom. There is a good deal of tea drunk, and coffee, and a vast amount of strong ale and porter; which all serve to induce more appetite for solid food. A man can eat two slices of bread and meat with a glass or a cup of liquid accompaniment, where he could use but one without. So the effect is apt to be excess; certain excess over the necessary amount of nourishment, probable excess over the wholesome point. In America, it is not the amount—although our women, as a rule, with their sedentary habits use too much, especially at breakfast time—but the kind of food, which makes the national deadly sin. Pies, cake, and hot biscuit, fried meat and doughnuts, pickles and preserves, bleach instead of reddening the blood; and except in some few districts we are a nation of anemics. If the unfortunate stomach can sustain the injury done it by lack of proper nourishment, it succumbs to the habit of bolting. Meal time is a succession of gulps and swallows grudgingly snatched from time devoted to the routine of labour, as hurried as nervous haste and the preoccupation of business cares can make it, and wholly unavailing for ordinary purposes of mastication. The unused teeth decay, and ruined digestion revenges itself in blanched cheeks, thinned hair, and general prostration. If this is too vivid a picture for the better knowledge and higher civilisation of our cities, it certainly is not for the country districts, and it is these last which produce the people. Towns may be the nerve ganglions, but the country supplies their forces.

The Parisian has changed all this. He begins the day with the slightest possible breakfast, leaving mind and body cleared, not weighted, for action. After three or four hours' work has induced a healthy demand for food, there comes a dainty and plentiful meal; two or three courses of meat, with a few vegetables, an omelette, bread and butter, fresh or prepared fruit. This answers to our lunch, and is usually served at noon or one o'clock. Six hours' later comes dinner. Soup always, often fish, four or five delicate and inviting preparations of meat, with a slight accompaniment of vegetables and some delicious sauce; a sweet, and a dessert of fruit and cheese form the points of this principal meal. Poorer families will have less, richer people will offer greater variety; but ordinarily this scheme very slightly modified will represent the daily routine of a Parisian household. For rich or poor the evening brings relaxation and social intercourse; to the one, in the dissipations and excitements of fashionable life; to the other, on the broad sidewalks of the boulevards, the animated brilliancy of the great Squares, the river embankments, the innumerable public resorts planned for the people. What wonder that life seems more a holiday here than in other places! The body remains alert and active; the power of enjoyment is unimpaired; the natural temperament does not suffer unnatural strain or twist. There is a pleasant mental as well as physical equipoise. It is a very grave question for those who desire to see temperance advanced —genuine temperance, and not some hobby of prohibition or total abstinence—whether the general use of the very light wines which are customary here would not be a solution of the difficulty. Our poor labouring people are intemperate in the use of bad tea and coffee, as well as of alcohol. The French workman takes his small glass of simple claret with his slice of bread and bit of meat. Physicians know that a large proportion of the physical ailments which come under their notice in America are aggravated even when they are not caused, by the daily bowls three times multiplied of weak and sloppy fluid which the labouring classes with us depend upon. In France there is nothing of the sort; and I am strongly inclined to believe it is a moral as well as a material blessing that the small quantity of wine takes its place. The entire plan of the French dietary system is better than ours; only that for the mass of Americans, accustomed to evenings at home and early bedtime, the order of the two principal meals might be reversed. Dinner could come at midday; lunch or supper toward evening. For the people abroad it is quite right as it is. Their evenings do not end before midnight, and they are filled with such movement and action as are in themselves helps to digestion.

These are some of the advantages the Parisian has over us in what might truly be called comforts. In the matter of luxuries and amusements, he leads the civilised world. Nowhere is entertainment of the senses and delectation of the mind so wonderfully catered for as in that marvellous city. The Government has lavished care, time, money, and the most exquisite taste upon the treasures without and within its public places, and then laid the keys where the lowliest as well as the loftiest hand can reach and use them. No wonder the pang of separation for one who is obliged to leave them is like the pang of death.

CHAPTER X.

THE WOMEN OF PARIS.

IF Paris is said to be the perfection of comfort, or nearly so, for man-kind, what is to be said of it for woman? Let us see. Taking first the profession which is still the most popular with the sex, in spite of the modern clamour for rights and opportunities, we shall find that the housewife has more amenities allowed in the carrying out of her ordinary duties than in most other portions of the world. The custom of having an apartment in a large hotel, instead of occupying the whole of a small house, lessens many of the trials of housekeeping. It can scarcely be necessary at this time to remind the reader that the French terms hotel and apartments are used in a sense quite unlike our own. Every large house built in many stories is a hotel, public or private; an apartment is one of the suites of rooms of which it is composed, with all the conveniences for housekeeping on whatever scale of size or luxury the purse permits or the taste dictates. It is almost precisely our system of flats—only that here it is universal. The concierge or janitor, on the lower floor, sees all visitors who enter the broad courtyard gate; attends to the halls, stairways, steps, windows, yard, and outside of the house; receives messages and bundles, calls a carriage, and does many of the simpler duties which relieve greatly the pressure of care in household arrangements. The washing is always done out of the house. The *blanchisseuse*, who comes for and returns it, lives usually out of town in some of the pretty suburbs, which give one assurance of at least plenty of fresh air in drying. There are numberless laundries through the city itself and in the great boats lining the banks of the Seine; but these are not so much patronised by families as by lodgers or boarders. So the damp cloud of washing-day disappears from the horizon of home. There is no baking of bread, cake, or pastry in the family kitchen. All that is relegated—as it should ever be—to professional bakers, who are the most admirable specialists. No one who has tasted the delicious little rolls which come with the morning coffee, or the sweet and wholesome long loaf which is cut in thick pieces for breakfast and dinner, will doubt the wisdom of thus replacing the so often wretched bread of America—left as it is to the half-trained judgment of the general servant. To be always perfectly sure of the bread and butter is to have won half the battle in providing a table. Here the butter, unsalted, and fashioned in dainty shapes, is as delicious as the rolls, and as invariable. There would be no hardship in making the principal part of the two daily meals, as well as the whole of the morning lunch, upon them.

The housekeeper and the cook also get rid of preparing the desserts. Nine times out of ten these are taken from the counters of the Pâtissier. The waiter in his full dress, the maid in her tidy cap and apron, or the mistress, if she is her own woman-of-all-work, looks about and chooses her tarts, or maccaroons, or eclairs, or whatever other form may be fancied, just before dinner is served, so that each article is as fresh and as good as it can possibly be. This, with a little fruit or conserve, is all; but any one who knows the variety and excellence of the cakes and pastry here knows that it is enough to satisfy the most exacting taste. The omnipresent salad, made from lettuce, or any similar green vegetable, and dressed simply with oil and vinegar, forms always one course, and to that extent helps to make matters easier. The morning cup of coffee, without the addition of anything save its accompanying roll, leaves the entire forenoon of each day free from preparations and clearing up of dishes—free, too, from the "planning" which becomes such weariness in the effort to devise new forms and combinations at home. The city is so exquisitely free from dust that there is no need of constant endeavour to prevent the accumulation of dirt, and so far as we have been able to find there is no spasmodic madness of spring and fall cleaning. The daily brushing, sweeping, and washing is found sufficient for daily needs; so that housekeeping, instead of being a fetish before whose altar blood and brains, nerves and strength are sacrificed, becomes rather a gracious and friendly power, whose worship is easy, and burden light. It is a kindly divinity instead of a dreaded juggernaut. Those who sneer at a people who have in their language no word for home should look rather at the spirit than the letter. They should note how the tiniest, poorest room, as well as the richest salon, is made less harsh by some comeliness, or neat curtain, or some cheap adorning; how the tradesman's wife and the labourer's bring back from their frugal morning marketing a blossoming spray or a green branch to lend its beauty to the one living room; how constantly the children, little and big, except in the case of the ultra fashionables, are by the side of the parents. They should see on afternoon or evening, Sunday or fête, according as occupation or circumstance allows, the family parties on the grass of the squares, in the free galleries, under the trees of the suburbs, crowding omnibuses or river boats—always happy, and always together. The daughter of thirteen is not enjoying herself with other young people; the son of fifteen is not learning the vapidness of life with a similar group of cigarette-smoking youths of his own age, with no watchful or prudent eye to offer remonstrance or suggestion. The cigarette is smoked, but it, like everything else, is *en famille*, and it would be extremely difficult for a conscientious observer to say that he has ever noticed that mirth was less hearty or youthful pleasure more hampered by this union of amusements and interests among fathers, mothers, and children. On the contrary, every face is keenly responsive.

As a natural consequence of this system the mother of the family finds more time at her command in which to associate herself with husband and sons. Among the poorer classes she employs this in sharing their labour: you find her sweeping crossings, sharing his duties as concierge or porter, by his side with some lighter portion of the work at the shoemaker's bench, the butcher's block, the tailor's table. Grown somewhat more prosperous, she takes her place behind the railing of the office desk and enters heartily into every interest connected with the business. I do not know whether French law recognises this same equality of partnership between the woman and the man, but most certainly French society does. One result is that, when sickness comes, or reverse, or death, the wife or mother is not the aimless, despondent, helpless being she is among us. At least her hands remain full, if her heart is empty of happiness. The consciousness of resource, the knowledge that she has the power to defy adversity, sustains and strengthens, and she is safely tided over the emergency. It is quite common to see in this way even large business interests continued by the wife alone or with her sons, or by the sister in connection with or succeeding her brothers. With us it is extremely rare, and many of the saddest changes in social position come from the absolute inability and ignorance of the woman which prevents her from grasping an opportunity. This is a phase in the rights and privileges of the sex which has been sadly neglected elsewhere, but which has been developed here with great success and mutual satisfaction, without any noise or confusion. Whatever may have caused a continuance of the custom, its inception at least must have been in large measure owing to the simplicity of arrangement which makes the actual management of the home so much easier an affair than with us.

Among the upper classes, the carrying out of the same principle gives the wife a proportionally large amount of time for other duties. If she is inclined to be charitable, or studious, or artistic, or worldly, there is plenty of opportunity to follow her bent. So we find the lady of fashion on the topmost round of the ladder of folly; the society leader gathering into her salons the wit, the wisdom, the politics, or the cabals of the capital; the student pushing thought and investigation into regions as yet remote, keeping pace with the masculine strength which usually leads the way; the artist surrounded by an atmosphere equal to that of any centre of impulse on the globe, with ancient tradition and modern achievement to spur her on. If there were forty different temperaments, each requiring one of forty different atmospheres in which to develop the highest possibilities, they might all find alike their moral and mental latitudes here. It is like one of those Alpine passes, down which in a few hours one travels through each grade of climate from the Arctic to the Tropics—only that this is of the spiritual order, while that belongs to the temporal. Of course, it is doubtful whether in the confusion of gaieties and interests, the average woman is not likely to allow herself to drift into the ways of least resistance, and to be simply wholesome and happy instead of having ideals and attempting a career. At the same time it is at least equally doubtful whether the average woman is not a greater success in this *rôle* than in any other, and whether it would not be quite as well for the world at large that she should forego any attempt at results which she can only fail to accomplish.

As for children, Paris comes as near paradise as earthly imagination can reach in fancying it. Imprimis, they are properly dressed here for the purposes of innocent amusement. The universal blouse of blue or black cotton covers each little form from fear of dust or soil, and leaves the dear, beautiful, dirty world free to dig and carouse in. They can spoil nothing. The quiet bonne or bright-eyed mother knits or embroiders, or gossips tranquilly with her neighbour, without that incessant chorus of nagging, half warning, half reproach, which spoils the pastime of our own darlings. At school, at play, at home, except during meal times, this blessed long apron, which covers such a multitude of virtues, does its beneficent work; and every child-loving heart is glad at sight thereof. To be sure, there are times, gala days and festivals, when it is laid aside, and Marie and Petite Pierre shine out in all the glory of baby finery; but this is only like the bon-bon. The other is the daily bread.

To one who loves children for their own sweet sake, there is much to be thankful for in the hint of absolute simplicity such attire as this gives. American babies are adorable; but they are as fragile as dolls, and almost as artificial in the silks and plushes, ribbons and laces of modern æsthetic requirement. Our young girls are much better dressed than in the old days when our volatile Gallic cousins complained, that no one walking behind an American maiden and her grandmother, could tell by the material or style of dress and decoration, which was which. There is a very delicate and exquisite taste shown in later years in the costuming of this younger portion of society. But the children are still overweighted with us, and the French apron offers the shortest way out of the dilemma.

Then there are the numberless localities prepared for their especial benefit. Scarcely a street of any size that has not its bit of flower-guarded, tree-shaded playground for the little creatures in its vicinity; not a single great pleasure ground that has not its ample proportion laid aside for the uses of this dear contingent. Gardens of the Luxembourg and Tuileries, the Champs-Elysées, enclosures of fountains, the lovely old church-yards, squares, places, courtyards, the Jardins des Plantes and d'Acclimatation, all have the children's portion jealously guarded for them from encroachment by the elders. Indeed, in most they are the absolute monarchs, and reign where and how they please. The beautiful Bois de Boulogne is an entire fairyland in itself. There are no lawns decorated with demands to keep off; there are no artificial beauties, which, like a painted cheek, will not bear the healthy ravages of natural causes without losing its sleek perfection; so the boisterous, roaming, happy hearts have it all their own way; to sail boats in the lakes, to run up hill and down dale, to tumble in the soft green of the long grass, to pick wild flowers until their small fingers weary of sweet labour, to do everything noisy and glad. But they are not noisy. The world goes so well with them that they can afford to be quiet.

When it comes to amusements of another kind, those to be paid for, and only enjoyed occasionally, they are still catered for on the same lavish basis. Here is the Hippodrome; a perennial circus, in a glass tent as large as three of Barnums, lifted eighty feet high, and showing day and night the most wonderful things that skill and daring can accomplish. Here are its bands of small jockeys in full hunting costume, mounted on ponies that would make the delight of any pair of eyes that ever twinkled in a boy's head, parading the streets every afternoon. Here in the Zoological Gardens is every animal that walks the earth, harnessed to triumphal chariots, which can be ridden for five cents, or stalking about the enclosures of their palaces, which can be seen for nothing. Here is Le Pays des Fées, where veritable fairyland waits behind the high walls, and where any child can walk through the enchanted gates into the regions where the Sleeping Beauty waits among the roses, where Hop o' my Thumb wins his victorious way through watchful cats and spiders, where Jack the Giant-killer and his namesake of the Beanstalk go through the magic of their traditional adventures, and where the two sisters drop jewels or toads from their lips as they wander by the fairy paths. Was there ever such delight to be bought before by pennies? And here again is the Gingerbread Fair, with its acres and acres of lanes covered with merry-go-rounds, captive balloons, flying horses, peep shows, mechanical toys, and every form of Cheap John that ever won a centime from a boy's or girl's pocket, with everywhere gingerbread adorned with comfits and frosting, painted with colours, stuffed with raisins, showered with nuts, streaked with citron, hot with spices, embroidered with tinsel, shining in gold and silver—so cheap! so cheap! So if Paris is not the children's paradise, there is no other reason than perversity. Not to mention eternal military bands, and endless files of shining, helmeted soldiers, and intermittent eruptions of flags and illuminations, which for one reason or another are constantly making day and night brighter than they are in the rest of the world.

Next to the children, the horse is the principal animal of Paris. He dominates the city much as the camel does Cairo. Off the side-walk there is no right which he and his appendage, the coachman, are at all bound to respect. Between his rampant aggressiveness as he drags about the 15,000 public and 20,000 private carriages, the brutal indifference of his driver, and the noiseless pavements of the broad streets, it is a miracle that in the busy portion of the day one ever gets across any of these wide thoroughfares alive. That one does is simply an intervention of benign Providence. Such reckless, dare-devil driving, such sudden sweeps and turns, such perfect indifference to the life and limbs of the poor, struggling, human mob, which is obliged to dodge and dash, and tremble between this pandemonium of horse flesh, it is impossible to imagine. There are raised stone platforms, erected at distances of thirty feet or so, to aid this flight for life, and the breathless hunted creature hurls himself upon these as a shipwrecked sailor would upon the last plank he sees floating by. There is no other security between him and annihilation. As for a woman! She looks up and down, before and behind; she clutches her skirts with a firm and nervous grasp; she makes a dash, only to be driven back before she has advanced five feet. She draws a long breath, tightens her hold, breathes a prayer, and tries again. Vain endeavour. She is under the nostrils of a fiery steed, that has spun around some unseen corner before her petticoats have left the curbstone. The third time despair and humiliation have made her furious; there is a dangerous gleam in her eye; she gives one glance of mingled wrath and defiance at a miscreant who is galloping toward her, and actually paralyses him into an instant's pause. *Io triumphe!* The next second she has reached the first halting-place. It is only a third of the distance, but she is there. A pause of a few minutes— well bespattered meantime by mud from flying hoofs. Again a hitch of the skirts; again a vain essay; another and another; then at last a new spasm of grim determination, a new mad dash into the gulf of difficulty and danger, a new access of moral courage as she mounts the second vestibule. This time Fate is kind; or it recognises beforehand that feminine diplomacy will finally be too much for it, and recedes from the unequal conquest. There are only four cabs, coming from four different directions, and a single cavalry officer bearing down upon her. She gives her head a toss! The harbour is in sight now, and she will reach it. She leaps in front of one, behind another, dodges a third by a splendid gymnastic *coup de théâtre*, the fourth turns up a side street, and the soldier pauses to salute a friend on the side-walk.

Glory to Allah! Hail to the Queen! She has passed the Rubicon! She has crossed the Champs-Elysées at four of the clock on a fine day, and she lives to tell it. But next time, let it be well understood, she takes a carriage. You think this is too highly coloured. Very well, Madame; wait until you try it yourself.

CHAPTER XI.

THE WAYS OF THE FRENCH WORLD.

SUCH a wise city! And such a foolish one! At a little dinner given yesterday to Jules Simon, there were around the table Barthélemy St. Hilaire, le Duc d'Aumale, Alexander Dumas, De Lesseps, Mezieres, Delibes, Gounod, and Meissonnier. Think what these men represent in the world of art, of music, and of letters. Yet the same city which they honour with their names and lives, goes *en masse* to the Wild West Show of Buffalo Bill, supposing that it is paying a compliment to the United States; and its highest officials from the President down, assist at the opening fête of this sublimated circus, as if by so doing they were honouring the sister republic. I am quite positive many of them considered the entire exhibition, bucking bronchos, cowboys, wild steers and all, as a representation of life in America, and the fringed leggings and red shirts of the dare-devil riders as the national dress. Indeed, more than one belle Marquise was heard to confide to her neighbour that the American costume was very picturesque. And here at the hotel, English as well as Frenchmen, recounting the novelties and wonders of the exhibition to their neighbours, speak of it as an "exact reproduction of life and manners in America." They think we put on civilisation only for travelling purposes.

No wonder the Parisians speak of being "tipsy" with the Boulevards. It is absolutely a species of intoxication

The life which whirls through them is so affluent in novelty, the interests they excite so various, that there is a sensation of dizziness and elation in the contemplation. One goes home tired, worn out with the swift passage of fancy from one novelty to the other; but with the first feeling of rest comes the desire for more. It is not like the incessant, tremendous maelstrom of London, which draws one in some greater or less degree toward a participation in the activity surging about; it is a milder and kindlier sentiment which admits the relaxation of observation without being driven to take part. One looks as one would at a picture—and what else is it? A movable picture; with a frame of soft shining, pale blue sky, in which one tableau succeeds another indefinitely. At one moment it is a company of mounted cuirassiers, in their shining helmets and long black plumes, coming under the great arches of the Louvre, and galloping away over Pont Neuf toward the towers of Notre Dame. The next it is some improvised market of fruit and produce, with picturesque hucksters in every variety of peasant cap and blouse, shrilling their wares under the trees like an encampment of gipsies. The next, one of the lovely gardens, within whose quiet paths flowers and children bloom, while pale statues and moss-draped monuments soften the glare of light and colour with the shadows of the centuries they have seen pass. Or the façade of some great public building, any one of a hundred of which, scattered as they are here among the intricacies of the narrow streets, would make one of our poor, wealthy American cities richer than all its millions. What it must be to live always where one can turn into the dim, cloistered mystery of Notre Dame, the jewel-like beauty of the Sainte Chapelle, glowing from floor to roof with that wonderful splendour of glass, which has no break save the carved spandrils of the Gothic arches that hold it; the dim, grand galleries of the Louvre, filled with the treasures which genius has left as heritage to time; the silent alleys of Père la Chaise, rich in the relics and haunted by the memory of the immortals! Among such surroundings, the present assumes its proper proportions. It is no longer the all-powerful and universal, it is but a point in a long vista, resplendent with such grandeur that it will take every force of nature and grace not to shame its ancestry of glory. It would be hard for such a world as this to become over-confident. Its own past is too tremendous an adversary.

To a stranger this charm is so strong that it is difficult to pierce it with the lance of reality. It takes something infinitely pathetic—like the little white coffin that passed to-day, borne under its wreath of flowers by two men, while one solitary mourner with bare, bent head walked behind—to bring the daily happenings of life here out of the realms of imagination and into those of the heart. Are these boisterous, showy joys, these heralded and uniformed sorrows real? Or is it all but a phase of the passing pageant introduced to give variety to the dramatic formula? If the visitor to whom these reflections come will get up some morning early, very early, many of these problems will solve themselves. It is a very real world which occupies the streets of Paris before the day of the ordinary inhabitant begins. Before seven o'clock the great markets have finished the largest portion of their buying and selling; the streets have been swept into that marvellous state of cleanliness that suggests dust-brushes and dust-pans as well as brooms; the different carts in the city's service have passed through lane and highway cleansing the unavoidable soil and scum which rise daily to the surface in the ways and means of life among half a million people. The fresh vegetables and flowers, brought in by countless country waggons, have left the streets faintly perfumed with spicy smells of growing green, freshly cut and dew-laden; milk-carts have made their noiseless rounds; coal and wood and any other form of bulk that could encumber the sidewalk have been delivered; the dirty work of that good housekeeper, Paris, is over for another twenty-four hours. What has seemed to your lazy eyes, opening ordinarily to the eight or nine o'clock sunshine, as a miracle, is simply a minute and exact division of labour, which has accomplished its wonders by perfectly natural means. You will see the waggons of the Board of Health lifting the heavy baskets of refuse by means of little windlasses at the back, and wish that the simple invention might be adopted by your own beloved but stupid country, where men are still obliged to hoist heavy barrels of dust and ashes by main force into tip carts higher than their heads. You will see water used like a flood to wash away every impurity; and thrifty housewives buying from peripatetic venders who carry loads of asparagus, of lettuce, or of carrots, daintily packed in fresh-cut grass, on their backs. You will hear the pipes of Pan, which have woven themselves into your morning dreams every day for months, coming up the street; and behold the gentle shepherd who plays upon them, leading his goats to milk at your door, into your own silver porringer, so that there shall be no fear of adulteration. What a pastoral symphony, with the sharp little click of the goats' hoofs beating time on the city pavement!

It gives one some insight into the enormous activity which underlies the apparent carelessness of French life, to see with what energy and satisfaction the smallest affairs are managed. One would scarce suppose the revenue obtained from the milk of five goats, driven each morning at dawn from a point miles outside the city, could be sufficient to satisfy the ambition of the man who sturdily travels before them. Yet it is the interest in just such small industries as this which has placed the country in that state of general prosperity which enabled it to overcome the cruel prostration following the Franco-Prussian War with such marvellous celerity. It was among farmers owning garden patches of half an acre, or a little flock of goats or sheep, or a few cows only, that the indemnity of millions demanded by the German Government was mainly taken up, without being obliged to call upon strangers for any part of the loan. No profit is too small, no occupation too lowly or minute to bring them happiness and honest pride in its pursuit; and so well have they comprehended Micawber's immortal formula of income and expenditure, that there is always a balance in their favour at the end of the year. Our people would scorn such slow and small profit, so that the weight of their indifference would soon begin to roll them and their affairs down-hill. These put such an earnest shoulder to the wheel that the burden must go up, and they with it. We have not yet learned how to distinguish the petty vexation of discontent, from the divine unrest of progress. We are afraid to do the small thing well, for fear we may thereby be induced to remain at it and lose an opportunity for some larger opening. The workman and workwoman here are as proud of the blouse and apron which are their marks of rank, as the gentleman is of his pedigree, and the lady of her salon. Their state is to them just as honourable.

The temper of the people, in regard to their rulers, may be gathered from this *jeu d'esprit*, which has lately had a wide circulation.

> "Carnot, montrez vous magnanime
> Pour ce Perrin ! Son attentat
> N'etait que l'ombre d'un crime
> Contre un ombre de chef d'état."

Which may be freely translated thus—Perrin being remembered as the name of the unfortunate idiot who attempted to fire at President Carnot on the day of the opening fête of the Exposition—

> "Carnot, be gracious! For this time
> Pardon Perrin. His fault in brief
> Was but the shadow of a crime,
> Against a shadow of a chief."

CHAPTER XII.

THE INVALIDES AND PÈRE LA CHAISE.

WHO that has ever thrilled at the name and fame of Bonaparte—and in spite of Carlyle's thunderbolts of denunciation, and the utilitarian spirit of the nineteenth century, how few there are that at some time have not!—can enter the portal of the dome under which he rests without a heightened pulse and some reflection of the old enthusiasm of youth? Outside in the sunshine of the paved court, with its walls of trees clipped into cool grottos of shadow, and its air of peace enhanced by the silent cannon which rest in bronze inactivity around the quiet paths, the old soldiers for whom the place was designed, sit with the peaceful shadows of the evening of life gathering about them. On their honourable breasts are the medals brought from many a desperate field; the neatness of military discipline is in every item of dress and carriage; the training of camp holds them erect before the advancing enemy of years. Those grizzled moustaches have faced death too many times to quail before his approach here. Any one of them, with brightening eye, will point your way to "Le Tombeau," the only tomb to those, who are its invincible Old Guard, stronger for their weakness than any pride or lustiness of manhood could make them. For them, almost as much as for that silent hero within, the struggles of life are over; for them, as for him, the beloved land, La Patrie, has provided a resting-place. Why should they not be content?

Inside, the great dome, with its pale blue light scarce piercing the lower shadows, rises above that grand sarcophagus, of which it seems the spiritual apotheosis. Looking down from the circular gallery at the dim vault below, the twelve colossal Victories which stand around the tomb with bowed heads, and crowns held in drooping hands, seem fit comrades for the dead commander. The barbaric glory of yellow mosaic which radiates from the centre of the floor is the only incongruous point in the dignity of conception of decoration. Why might they not have allowed the green laurels of the inner wreath to tell their own story, with Marengo and Austerlitz, Rivoli and Jena lending their brilliant names to bind them together? Why might they not have left those eloquent trophies—the tattered flags snatched from the proudest and strongest hands of Europe?—to speak for him. With this sombre stone as a centre, there is no need of spur for the imagination. One likes to think of him here safe from the tortures of that living death, or the cruel rock that held him so long from the land and the people, which in spite of all his errors of impetuous ambition he loved so well. If it were only for the impulse he gave to the material beauty of France, and for the unusual clearness and justice of many of his terse edicts of military law, the country has reason never to forget his memory, nor forego its meed of honour to him. Women especially should remember with kindliness one who was first to make the wife's rights equal to the husband's in the division of property; giving her such complete control of one entire half of their mutual possessions, that she could dispose of it in any way she pleased without his consent. In the partnership of marriage he considered the housekeeper's work, with its ceaseless activity, thrift, devotion, and helpfulness, equal to the exertions of the breadwinner in forming a foundation of prosperity;

and he gave to the woman a legal right to her share of the results. It was a magnanimity of understanding and of action to which the rest of the world has not even yet attained; and it should be remembered for Bonaparte, at least as long as his impudent rejoinder to Mme. de Stael's impudent question, which is so often used as a stone to fling back at him. "The evil that men do lives after them," and with perfect justness; but let us see that the good remains also to lessen the shadow of reproach.

It is sincerely to be hoped that a day may come when the great museum of the Invalides, with its chronology written in instruments of blood, may be regarded as we now do the mechanisms of torture belonging to the Inquisition. These illustrations of the long, dark chapter of history, which records human weakness and cruelty, should be as out of date in these days of progress as the coarse woodcuts of the Middle Ages. The leaf is not yet turned which will relegate them to the past and make them wholly matters of impersonal curiosity, but its time is as surely approaching as that of to-morrow's sunrise. Every dome and spire that glistens beyond there in the Champs de Mars* is a hand raised to heaven against the wickedness of war and desolation. The people who see before them such evidences of the wealth, the nobility, and the magnificent strength of labour, will not be long in questioning the principle which turns its power into weakness and its riches into dust. May the time come soon which is to change every injustice of force into the holy uses of the brotherhood of mankind.

After the Invalides, one naturally turns toward Père la Chaise, where lie so many of Napoleon's comrades. Next to the magnetism of contact with the living personage is that of standing by his tomb. Wandering here amid these

* The Exposition buildings.

serried ranks of the great ones of the earth, a species of exaltation seizes one. The most leaden fancy cannot help but rise somewhat to the level of the spiritual company in which it finds itself. Here are they who moved nations and changed the face of the world, some with the shock and crash of arms, some by the brilliant light of genius, some by the quiet force of patient and loving endeavour. Père la Chaise, more than the Pantheon, is the Westminster Abbey of France. What a grouping of the Immortals! The Marshals of France, that dazzling band that flashes like a train of comets across the battlefields of centuries; soldiers and sailors, sculptors, artists, poets; doctors who have lightened the woes of mankind, and politicians who have often added to them; authors and actors; scientists and mathematicians; all names that are like the voices of old friends heard again after long absence. One can fancy the leaders of each group surrounded by their followers. Ney and Massena, Lefebvre and Bruat, David and Corot, and Alfred de Musset. Here would be Nélaton and Larrey, De Morny and Thiers, Racine, Balzac and La Fontaine, Molière and Rachel, Gall and La Place. What an acre of the gods! To one who walks amid these close-built paths for the first time the shadow of these great names is almost as constant as that of their resting-places. Turn as one may, some ray of glory flashes from the darkest corner. But why could they not have left the poor, outworn bodies to the light of day and the soft, warm covering of the sod, instead of those cumbering weights of marble and granite? Why should the imprisonment of the spirit instead of its emancipation still be kept before our eyes by these ugly piles of stone and mortar? But perhaps the poor ghosts would not feel at home released from the sombre twilight of barred doors and grated windows. Certainly Père la Chaise would not be half so picturesque. The names over the dark thresholds of this little city of dead Paris outshine all the pride of the living, although they are so often the same. Each of the families that glitter in the sunshine of life beyond, whose palaces resound with the triumphant accompaniments of wealth and fame, has here its small house of retirement and rest, where at last peace may be found, and silence. No matter how burning the loves and hates, the ambitions and failures of yonder world, here is the quiet of eternity to ease the bruises of time. Perhaps green fields and the tender voice of Nature might not speak their lesson so loudly.

It will be many weeks before the attractions which so powerfully hold one within the city fortifications relax sufficiently to allow any normal interest in the world beyond the walls. But when at last, native curiosity or the representation of friends induces you to cross the Rubicon, another little rap on the knuckles by one of the anachronisms of Paris awaits you. Here is in many respects the centre of the world's civilisation. Here is the focus from which the rays of highest progression in thought, in art, in science, in every form of cultivated labour, spread themselves to the ends of the earth. There is no improvement of modern times which has not been availed of to make the city beautiful, shapely, strong. She has thrown aside the shackles of ancient custom, and resplendently arrayed herself in the garments of Freedom. Yet outside every gate that leads from her broad avenues into the country beyond, is a relic of the intolerance and ignorance of the dark ages in a wretched little Custom House whose officers poke their hands into your travelling satchel, and their noses into your business, to see that you are carrying no article for sale or barter from one town to another without paying first the duty upon it. Here is Protection carried to its logical conclusion. To keep the home market for the home consumer, a gardener may not sell a bunch of radishes, of which he has too many, to his neighbour who has too few, simply because the neighbour's house is within the line of another township. You drive to the town of Vincennes; a liveried official hands you from the carriage, eyes your suspicious handbag or lunch-basket, and makes you empty it before him or not, according to his discretion and the state of his digestion. A market waggon passes into St. Mande on the way; other officials fumble among the baskets of eggs, the piles of carrots and cabbages, until their estimate is made, and the privilege of entrance paid for. You go to the Forest of Fontainebleau by train or diligence, to the Palace of Versailles, or Asnières, or Marly le Roi, or La Malmaison; always the same formal etiquette of apprehensiveness for fear that a sou's worth of contraband material is concealed in your woman's one pocket or your man's twelve. And you are always absolutely placed in a position where a right of search can be exercised upon you in the name of the law, and where you are quite powerless to prevent or resent it. And these are the gates of Paris at the end of the nineteenth century; and the Government which has taken down the mottoes of faith and love from the portals of their churches to surmount them by the legend of *Liberté, Egalité, Fraternité*, sees no incongruity in this miserable hodge-podge on equal rights in trade and barter. Not content with placing obstacles in the way of the adventurous foreigner who would cross their boundaries with merchandise, they obstruct the progress of their own people in the same way. The wonder is that they do not place one of these invisible barriers between the twenty-eight different arrondissements of the city; and deny the Quartier Latin the privilege of buying or selling to the Champs Elysées, or the opposite.

It is to be hoped this remnant of mediæval stupidity will not prevent your roaming about through those exquisite suburbs; after all, Paris needs some faults as well as some follies to make it human. There is no point to choose which has not its own special attraction, and in which loving care has not added to historic value. So that some day will probably find you at St. Cloud, walking toward Sèvres through the marvellous park, which is certainly one of the most beautiful, as it is one of the smallest, of the royal pleasure-grounds of ancient France. Keep, if you are wise, the broad, green alleys under the trees, under the terraces of fountains, with glimpses of chateaux and soft grey spires between the vistas; with groups of statuary, and gracious figures of bronze and marble showing here and there beyond leafy arches, with the prattle of children and the ripple of bird voices making the sweet air melodious. And go instead to the other Palace of Industry, which hides under the trees at one corner by the river gate of Sèvres. So small a place to be so world famous! Go to the Museum, where everything in grace and beauty in ceramics, which the genius of man has produced in any country or civilisation, is gathered, as a clinic for the imagination which is to study form and colour from them. See the school for the artist and designer which this freely unlocks, so that his efforts may be quickened in the right direction and march from greatness to greatness. You will not wonder, then, at the marvellous strides which this manufactory has taken in artistic rank, or why it holds its place with the foremost conceptions of modern skill.

Behind the exhibition rooms, filled with an infinity of objects of more than regal magnificence, a very courteous official, in uniform and white gloves, leads you through the workshops. There are the lumps of white clay, cleansed and sifted; and the pulverised glittering silicate which makes the dough for the biscuit. There is the infinite care with which it is mixed and kneaded until the consistency is at just the proper degree. There is the moulding in so many delicate pieces, or the modelling upon the potter's wheel of objects so fragile that a breath would be sufficient to crush them. There is the separate fashioning of the handle of the dainty cup and its foot; the preparation of the enamel and its application; the frameworks which are to support the frail body until it has been hardened by the test of fire. There are the mighty ovens, roof high, within which the tender handiwork is piled; each tiniest bit in its own separate compartment; the sealing up of doors and chinks with moist clay; the huge fires in which scores of cords of wood blaze and smoulder; the gradual cooling off; the anxious search for failures and imperfections. And then the decoration, in which trained eyes and hands apply the most delicate touches with such infinite care that the simplest band seems an endless task; and the second firing, to burn the dull colours into beauty and brightness; and the burnishing with polishing tools, which gives the last touch or finish. And there at last is your simplest cup that leaves the workshop of Sèvres; deep with that rich blue which glows like some strange jewel, framed in a rim of shining gold as delicate as frostwork; perfect with the perfection of educated human skill rather than the clumsy exactness of machinery. Of course, you carry it home as a trophy and place it among your Lares and Penates to speak to you for ever of a summer holiday under the deep arches of the forest of St. Cloud, and a few hours of absorbing interest spent in watching one of the highest developments of trained labour. If you have ever wondered before why Sèvres cost so much, you will restore the balance hereafter by wondering how it can cost so little. According to all the rules of recompense, according to the time and taste, the imagination and training lavished on your one tiny cup and saucer, instead of three dollars, it should have been bought with three hundred.

CHAPTER XIII.
ON THE EIFFEL TOWER.

I WONDER if one could ever leave Paris without regret, whether it were years or months that had made it familiar. There are some forms of beauty for which no familiarity can breed contempt, and this fair city seems to possess them. The last night, as we stood under the shadow of the Arc de Triomphe, while the great revolving light atop of the Eiffel Tower bathed us now and again in a blaze of white radiance, it seemed as if nothing made by hand of man could be more glorious. Down the long length of the Champs Elysées, close lines of large lamps stood like torch-bearers under the trees reaching to the obelisk; between them, a maze of moving sparkles, like swarming fireflies, filled the broad way, as the lighted carriages went and came. On either side, separated by the leafy shade which arched over broad side-walks, the tall stately palaces shone with faint gleams from balconied windows, as the night air moved lace draperies enough to show the rosy and amber glory of the silken shaded lights within. Behind us, the equally beautiful Bois de Boulogne melted into the darkness, with its long train of torches again holding place as guard of honour; with its own host of moving carriage lamps, and façades of houses gleaming white under the silver shining of the moon. A mob of foot-passengers, with that expansive gaiety and careless ease which mark the Parisian always, but more especially in the evening, lounged over the smooth flags which would almost mask the tread of an army; and the brilliant equipages as they rolled by showed whatever was most elegant in the dress and form of fashion. It was like some grand fête; and such it is, only that the festival goes on for ever.

We had gone in the morning to the Eiffel Tower, as it was the first day on which the upper lifts had been opened to the public. Ten minutes after the doors in the great corner masses of masonry were thrown open, five hundred people were in line at the station which conveyed passengers to the second stage, from which the final ascent is made. Two flights of stairs led up to what appeared to be a small house of two stories, each consisting of a single room with doors and windows. Immediately on entering, the house and the fifty or sixty persons in it began to move diagonally up the three hundred feet of inclined plane leading to the first platform. Less than five minutes sufficed to land one at this preliminary stage, which proves to be an enormous hollow square, filled by four large restaurants and numberless smaller booths for the sale of different articles. Over the balustrades which protect the open centre and the outer promenade, one saw the city as a bird might, not yet too far away to destroy the symmetry of proportion and the relative effects of height and distance. From this point the Exposition grounds were singularly attractive; the paths among the pleasure gardens and the lovely lanes full of strange pavilions, kiosks, minarets, pagodas, and temples being perfectly outlined.

Numbers were already breakfasting in the Russian Tea House, or the Alsace and Lorraine Café, where pretty girls in the picturesque costume of their country dashed in and out with jingling piles of plates and glasses. The space covered in was so vast, and the number of shops so large, that it was as if a village had been suddenly lifted into the air and planted there. A forest of flags and streamers rose from gable and roof-line, while a close line of lamps outlined the entire outer edge, so as to produce the girdle of fire we see by night.

It was considered more exciting to climb to the next stage, two hundred feet above, so we tried it. The stairs are like long narrow corkscrews, bolt upright, connected by five flights of steps in the ordinary fashion. These teetotums are fortunately guarded by high iron fences, so tall that one's head barely reaches above, so that unless one makes an effort to become dizzy there is no opportunity for such nonsense. Neither was there any foundation for the reports of swaying, sea-sickness, and insecurity, which float about the lower world in regard to the ascent. It was as immovable and firm as a mountain-side. The tiresomeness of the climb was more than repaid by the novelty as one wound in and out amid the lacework of light iron which crossed in every direction like threads of a spider's web. The second stage, when reached, was still very large. *Figaro* had a printing office there, and books to receive names and addresses which were regularly published in the evening edition. There were more booths, more cafés, more side-shows, but the view was practically unchanged. The towers of Notre Dame and the Trocadero seemed to have flattened somewhat, and one could look farther into the suburbs; that was all.

Now came the final tug. We entered with some threescore others into a fair-sized room, with walls half made of windows, and immediately began to go up, perpendicularly this time, and very slowly. In a few minutes came a halt; a door opened on one side, through which all passed into another room precisely similar, and the ascent began again. It was found to be safer that the last five hundred feet should be divided into two stages, so that too much strain should not be put on cables and machinery. A few moments more of somewhat heightened expectancy; the slow motion ceases; and one steps out into a large square gallery wholly enclosed with glass. It is capable of holding perhaps four hundred people, and one is obliged to wait until reason has forced imagination into a belief in fact before one even looks out. It seemed preposterous that this hall should be the little platform swung like an eagle's nest in the air that we had been looking at for weeks at the top of the tower.

Then we looked down. The lower earth had become a toy world like a large-sized Noah's Ark. There were swarms of dolls moving in every direction. Some carried umbrellas as big as toad-stools; some rode in carriages with horses the size of Newfoundland dogs. One baby doll walking between two elders was merely a speck of white, beneath which two black points shot out alternately in steps twice as large as the little body. There were toy boats gliding here and there under arches of the river; a company of toy soldiers marched as if moved by a spring across the bridge of Solferino; a squad of cuirassiers, their brass helmets shining like pins' heads in the sun, moved over the square before the military school. The brave gilt halberdiers on the roof of the Hotel de Ville shone too; so did the Dome of the Invalides. The Exposition buildings had shrunk to the size of dwelling-houses; the dwelling-houses to that of cabins. The horizon stretched in a radius far beyond Fontainebleau and Versailles. The low hills which ordinarily bound vision had sunk to mounds; and the city faded—faded from the solid white mass of its central portion to scattered faint colour in the environs, and strong green beyond. The Bois de Boulogne was a large field with clumps of trees; the great flower-beds in the grounds and the Trocadero Gardens were decorations for some fine dinner-table. The large marble groups were parian statuettes. By leaning far out one saw the white tables in the restaurants on the grass below, like ladies' small handkerchiefs spread out to dry. It was all unreal, as if you and your companions were Brobdingnagians, looking down upon some town of little Gullivers. And although the wind would have blown you into space were it not for the protecting interposition of the walls, there was but the faintest possible tremor, so slight that one should lean heavily against the side to be conscious of it at all. It was an experiment no one would like to have left untried, if it were only to have gotten that exquisite glimpse of the silver-grey Seine winding in large slow curves under the beautiful arches of its score of bridges.

The Parisians, always on the alert for a new sensation, have seized upon this ascent of the Tower with a species of frenzy. Partly a national pride in the success of their countryman's great work, partly the harmless intoxication one feels in the rarer medium of a higher atmosphere, draws them by thousands to the mild audacity of the attempt. The height and the novelty are still the source of never-failing wonder and delight to the hundreds of thousands who visit the grounds daily. "But that is a tower! Mon Dieu! How it is beautiful! I go to ascend it." "Thou, Alphonse? What, to the top?" "Yes, to the top. It will be cheaper soon on Sundays and fêtes. But cheap or dear, I go!" "How thou art brave! I—I would die of fear before I reached the second platform." By the time the Exposition is over, there will probably be neither man nor gamin in Paris, who can beg, borrow, or steal the necessary five francs, that will not have connected himself by this bit of personal experience with the glory of Eiffel and his colleagues. These last have combined prudence with enterprise in a remarkable degree. They expect—and it is more than probable from present appearances that their expectations will be realised—to clear by ascensions alone a sum of 2,000,000 francs during the next five months, over and above the original cost. If afterward, as is vaguely rumoured, the structure should be removed and set up in a permanent position, it would remain indefinitely a source of permanent income. Beside, there is the revenue from the rental of the four great restaurants erected on the first platform, three hundred feet up, to which the cost of ascent is very trifling, and from which a superb view of city and suburbs can be obtained. It is an ideal place for dinners, and the "little suppers" of which the people are so fond. It is not wholly, then, of the honour of France and the adorning of its centennial celebration of Liberty that Eiffel was thinking. But surely no American can throw the first stone at him for this.

CHAPTER XIV.

ORLEANS.

AFTER one has seen this portion of country which stretches toward the middle of France, through the valley of the Loire, it is hard to understand why it should be considered wanting in the element of the picturesque. The low, billowy hills which cease almost immediately after passing the immediate environs of Paris, give place to a series of limitless plains, beautiful, fertile, and so flat that the horizon is like that of the ocean. There is neither stone wall nor hedge to break the continuity, yet there is no sense of sameness in the boundless outlook. Every form and variety of grain and produce finds rich harvest ground in these sunny fields, broken only by occasional groups of the stately poplars so peculiar to France, or the orchards about the grey piles of peasant buildings. Splendid dashes of colour are given by masses of flame-red poppies among the wheat, and patches of brilliant yellow mustard stretching here and there between the green growths. Now and again near the roadway, or far in the distance, the pointed terra cotta roofs of a village shine dully amid the trees; or the strangely complicated groups of buildings enclosing the courtyard of some isolated farm give that peculiar foreign effect which is so dear to the traveller. The streams which water this lovely valley, even when not visible to the eye, can be traced by the winding lines of trees which mark their course; and the numberless variations in the crops, which seem to embrace every known species of vegetable, give such gradations of tint, that the eye is soothed rather than fatigued. Every inch of the large farms is kept with the care which might be expected in a small market garden, and the immediate neighbourhood of the house is usually brightened by flowers. When, as one travels farther, the vineyards begin, with their strange expanses of short, bare poles, about which the young vines are only beginning to climb, it is still saved from monotony by the constant recurrence of the cultivated fields, with their crops for home consumption.

The farm buildings are so strange to the traveller that they merit a word of description. Built always of stone, usually covered with coarse mortar, and arranged around a large courtyard paved with cobble-stones, the long, low houses, with their steep gables, have an aspect of solemnity, from the absence of windows, which is out of harmony with their smiling surroundings. Whether it is economy, or some strange perversity in regard to the uses of sunlight, or simply another form of the distemper which causes the New England farmer's wife to pull down her curtains, close her blinds, and live in the dark, I do not know, but the average farm-house here is built as if the sun were a criminal to be kept out with bolts and bars. It is quite probable that the occupants, women as well as men, live so much in the open air, that the house is simply a place to eat and sleep in, so that the want is not felt as with us. Certainly their colour is better, and there is more vivacity in their movements than among our tired, pale people. The barns, stables, corn and out-houses all open on the same court as the dwelling, but there seemed to be no accumulation of dirt or untidiness on that account. In this portion of France, at least, the cleanliness of town and country is very striking. When one remembers the filth which disfigured the cabins in those beautiful Irish fields, one is forced to believe that the difference in system which makes the Frenchman his own landlord, and the Irishman only a tenant at the will of a careless absentee, must have something to do with the change.

Orleans, after Paris, is like dropping into the sixteenth after having been in the twentieth century. The strangest feeling of antiquity possesses one upon entering. The narrow paved passages, with high, sombre houses frowning down, look more like ways inside the walls of a fortress than streets of a city. Stone and masonry are so beneath and about that the reality of a time of warfare is constantly forced upon the mind. Even the squares, though sunny, are not bright and cheerful. Everywhere are reminders of the Maid of Orleans, and the time to which she belonged. Shops of every possible description are named after her. Jewellers reproduce her face, her figure, her shield, in their ornaments. Stationers fasten them into their penholders and paper weights. Art galleries place her pictures and statuettes before everything else in their collection. You can even order a dress of silk or muslin after her colours and devices at the drapers, or eat her bodily in ice, in cake, or in chocolate bon-bons at the confectioners. Her statue is in half-a-dozen places. In the Hotel de Ville is a bronze copy of the design executed in marble by the Princess d'Orleans; a dignified and beautiful conception, doubly valuable as coming from the hands of a woman. In the Place Martroy a fine equestrian statue, cast in bronze from nine cannon, disappoints one on a closer investigation by the aimless expression of the face, which is that of a pretty girl posing in a masquerade. The sixteen bronze bas-reliefs set within the pedestal of granite are of great force and beauty, giving, as they do, a summary of the principal scenes in the heroine's life. On the bridge of the Loire is the statue cast in 1804 by Gois, where she is represented leading on foot, with

II

drawn sword and uplifted banner, the charge against the English. In this the face and figure might have been copied from Mary Anderson; and the pose, full of action, yet wanting in some indefinable way the element of sympathy, suggests our American girl also. It is precisely the way Miss Anderson would "create" Joan of Arc. Not far away a paltry cross mounted on an uneasy pillar marks the spot where the memorable charge upon the tower or Fort des Tournelles, was made on the 7th of May 1429. An earlier statue erected by the women of France in 1458 was unfortunately melted into cannon during the Reign of Terror, but the copy preserved in the museum is so extremely ugly that regret for its loss can be only on historic grounds.

The same museum, which is entirely devoted to her memory, contains some rare old Flemish tapestries, representing the different events in her career of arms, numberless paintings and statuettes in wood, bronze, and metal, showing her in every conceivable attitude and circumstance, from the time of the visions at Domremy to the martyrdom at Rouen, and a most interesting collection of bas-reliefs and etchings. Among the potteries is a plaque of Palissey ware, on which she is shown drawing the arrow from her neck at the moment when she falls wounded, in accordance with her prophecy, before the battle outside the walls. A number of arrow-heads in flint, stone, and crude iron, with some of the balls thrown from the English mortars—stone, and as large around as a man's body—are also here, with the banner which was painted by Leonardo da Vinci, and which has been carried in the annual procession since the time of Francis I. It is impossible to obtain any clear view of the heroine's face or figure after studying these relics. She is presented in every phase, from that of the simple dreamer to the triumphant warrior, and each conception is utterly unlike. Some are heroic, some shrinking, some wasted by fasting and prayer, others superbly alive with consciousness of power; some make her blonde, others brunette. One must select for himself.

That Circe of a Paris, which turns the head of all who have partaken of her hospitality, and makes all beauty seem paltry beside her own, prevents one at first from doing justice to Orleans. Yet the city is attractive in a new, half-sullen fashion. The tortuous, strangely winding streets open in the most unexpected spots upon houses of great architectural beauty and historic value, like that of Agnes Sorel or Francis I. Some quarters, like those about the old church of St. Paul, are as if they still remained in the Middle Ages. An isolated belfry and a high convent wall on one side, and the church itself upon the other, bound a paved lane which twists and turns between cobbled sidewalks not two feet wide, with vistas down other dark ways, like dungeons which have been opened on top to light and air. Such a network of corners and curves, such strange massive greystone houses, such gloomy arches opening into gloomy courts, such tiny dark shops. You feel that a post chaise and four or a canopied sedan chair should be the means of locomotion instead of that noisy tramway yonder, with its shrill whistling conductor on the front platform. The cathedral, which is very fine, strongly reminds one of Notre Dame, both without and within, although it is so much smaller; but it has too many windows, and so lacks the impressiveness of the older and greater church. The high altar, which was a gift of Louis XV., the windows at the end of the nave, and some of those in the lateral chapels, and an exquisite piece of sculpture in purest Carrara marble to the memory of the beloved Bishop Dupanloup, are its greatest ornaments. The exterior is noted for the finely carved front façade, and the delicacy of the flying buttresses at the side. There is not one of the old churches which is not beautiful and interesting. Under that of Saint Aignan extends a crypt constructed by Charlemagne. To those who have been bred in the belief that all the religious persecution of the Middle Ages was the work of Catholics, it is somewhat novel to find the desperate spirit of vandalism which disfigures history during the years when the Protestants found themselves in power. The cathedral was razed to the ground in 1567; St. Aignan, within a year from that time; St. Enverte was ravaged and pillaged by them, and most of the other churches of Orleans felt their fury. There seem to be two sides to every story.

Out in the direction of Olivet, one of the nearest suburbs of the city, are the sources of the Loiret—a charming bit of landscape beauty. One passes for a few miles along a white country road, enclosed on each side by enormously high walls, white too, and only occasionally broken by the gable end of a house built into them, or an orchard and bolted gateway. If any one of these openings chances to be ajar, one sees within acres of flowers and gardens, where the city florists produce their beautiful wares, and an odour of acacias, of roses, of pansies, perfumes the air. Sometimes a straggling vine, heavy with blossoms, nods over some gap in the enclosures, or a few trees throw a grateful shade over the dazzling way. But until the bridge of Olivet is reached there is very little shelter. Here one descends to the river bank through the pretty garden of Eldorado, and takes the boat for the head of the river, some two miles away. The rowers pull under the greystone arches and out into a stream which is lined on either side with trees and villas of the quaintest description. Built of brick or stone, with an arched opening of masonry below, into which the water flows, and where the pretty pleasure-boats of the family are moored, there is above but a single room, with its large window or windows opening on a balcony which overhangs the river. The door is toward the land side; a little garden planted thickly with flowers and shrubbery separates the tiny domicile from its neighbour, and a narrow flight of stone steps leads to the water's edge. Here on Sundays and holidays the merchants of the city come to enjoy the hours of summer idleness; and such fairy spots for rest and recreation never were seen before. They are just summer houses, not much bigger, with all their surroundings, than a child's playground, and furnished with the most coquettish grace. Here and there a real country house breaks the quaint uniformity, like the Chateau de La Source, in whose prim gardens Voltaire read his Henriade to Lord Bolingbroke in 1722. But nothing is so fascinating as these tiny pleasure homes, rising like a miniature and rural Venice from the tree-shadowed, beautiful river, which flows so tranquilly full of emerald light under their flower-hung balconies. There can scarce be another such picturesque nest in the world.

Orleans is a centre for many forms of industry. There are here potteries, manufactories of pins, corsets, woollens, iron bedsteads, immense refineries, whose products are exported all over Europe, and large establishments for wine and vinegar. When you taste the very large bottles of very small vin ordinaire which are served with your excellent dinner and breakfast at any of the little inns with the big names Le Grand Hotel d'Orleans, for instance—you will surely think they have confounded these two products, and given you the vinegar instead of the wine. It would be an admirable drink in the interests of temperance, for, like the Mexican pulque, very little is enough. The city, besides having been at all times a favourite resting-place of the ancient kings of France, and enriched by them with numberless gifts of treasure and public buildings, the remains of which can be seen to this day, has been further made glorious by being the birthplace of Robert the Pious; Bongars the historian; Etienne Dolet, the learned printer and martyr, in whose honour a statue has just been raised at Paris; the great jurisconsults Pothier and Jousse, as well as many others. It was the seat of the ministries of St. Euverte, St. Aignan, St. Prosper, St. Eucher, the learned prelate Theodulphe, and the no less revered Monseignor Dupanloup, who in different centuries were bishops of the cathedral. But for those who go to it from the outside world, it is for its frowning, gloomy streets; its reminiscences of the young life of the heroine of France; its beautiful, though few, churches; and its smells—which are neither few nor beautiful—that it will be best remembered.

CHAPTER XV.

BLOIS.

It is small wonder when Tasso, who knew the town and the people well, praised Blois so quaintly in his Jerusalem Delivered, that one who has seen it but through the happy span of a midsummer holiday should do likewise. Tasso often effected the rare combination of sense with poetry, but never more truly than in this case. It is the most charming spot in the beautiful valley of the Loire, set on the right of the river bank on a group of small steep hills which make the only break in the flat plains that extend on every side for thirty miles above and below it. It is rather one hill and a couple of terraces, but the effect is the same. It is easy to imagine that this superiority of location would make the place important in those early ages when might ruled the world; and as matter of fact, the fortress, which formerly occupied the place of the present chateau, was built upon the ruins of an ancient Roman fortified camp. When religion came to add its greater strength to that of men and arms, and in the sixth century the body of St. Solenne, which was being conveyed from Luynes to Chartres, stopped of its own accord at the hill of Blois, and refused to be carried further, nothing remained but to build a church about the sacred relics, and leave them at the spot for which they had shown so decided a partiality. Sanctity as well as misery loves company, and the Benedictines soon brought the body of their good Saint Laumar to the same place, to become the nucleus of one of the most famous and splendid abbeys of the Middle Ages. Pilgrims and strangers from all parts of the kingdom naturally gathered about the spot which offered them at once spiritual and temporal security, and the little town increased in years, in grace, and in numbers, until the birth of King Louis XII., in 1462, within its walls, gave the finishing touch to its greatness. The wars which so continuously desolated the rest of France seemed to spare this favoured retreat, until the religious struggles of the sixteenth century, and the controversy for supremacy between Henry III. and the Duke of Guise, made it the centre of intrigue between Catholics and Huguenots. In terrible contrast to the peace and prosperity which marked the years when the kindly Louis had decreed liberty of worship according to conscience, and declared free from all taxes, whether of war or peace, revenues destined to buy books, pictures, or treasures of such like sort for the great library he founded in his beloved château, were the scenes of violence which followed. Guise was murdered here; and here also, during the fêtes offered by Charles IX. and the Queen mother to the Calvinist leaders, the horrors of the massacre of St. Bartholomew were plotted. For the thirty years following this time, until Henry IV. made Paris the actual, as it had been the nominal, seat of power, Blois was really the capital of France. Afterward, although it knew the presence of Richelieu and Marie de Medicis, although kings and dukes flew to it and from it in pursuance of political schemes, although the Grande Monarque, Louis XIV., enlivened it with the sun of his presence, the Château of Blois fell more and more into decay and disuse. The Revolution mutilated it and scattered the few remaining glories which the rapacity of greedy royalty had left. It was only in 1845 that the Government of France voted money to restore the beautiful and historic ruin. The work is now almost wholly finished;

only a small portion of one wing being yet in process of construction. The rest of the building is in the perfect condition in which Francis the First and Louis the Gentle left their favourite abode.

Figure to yourself, as our cousins—not cousins-German, but cousins French—are fond of saying, the Blois of to-day. The principal part of the town being built on the lower level and surrounded by forests, the towers of the churches and roofs of the chateau are almost all one sees as the railroad from Paris approaches. A broad and beautiful boulevard has been constructed, opening up the middle of the city, well paved, and turning into the equally broad and beautiful highway which passes over the stone bridge crossing the Loire. Remarkably pretty houses, dazzling white, with stone or plaster façades, and charming balconies of wrought and gilded iron outside the long windows, border this fine promenade on either side. The shops and restaurants on the street floors are the brightest we have seen in any spot outside Paris itself. Indeed, with its lovely little square and fountain at one end, under the lofty terraced wall of the chateau, and its broad, clean, shining sidewalks of flags, this portion of it irresistibly recalls the capital. But the blue, bright, high-arched sky, and the beautiful wind-blown swallows darting in swift flight around the eaves and gables from morning until night, are better than even Paris. You saunter along the promenade admiring the faience of Blois in the shop windows, the enormous cherries and strawberries in the market waggons, the cheery and pleasant faces which seem to offer you a good wish in passing. Suddenly an opening on the left, not bigger than a medium-sized doorway, allows you to look up a street—a pathway—as steep and as narrow as a staircase, which twists itself out of sight among its dark stone houses before it has gone two hundred feet. You walk on filled with delight, as if you had had a glimpse

into a world three centuries back. Suddenly again another
opening just as steep, just as narrow, just as dark, but a real
flight of steps this time, springs up, with two sunny-haired boys
and a little black goat in the centre of the paved way. "The
little ladder of St. Honoré" is this; and the quaint name is as
pretty as the quaint situation. A few steps farther on, just
across the street, a passage opens on the left; down it goes,
as deeply as the others, dipping here and there under archways, sombre as twilight in the midst of noonday. And now a
stone staircase, semicircular, 50 feet broad, with a sunny plot
of flowers in the middle, and flowering acacias shading each
side, sweeps upward in a set of terraces a hundred feet or
more above the street, level to a rampart-like wall which rises
above the chimneys. Slowly you climb, the flying swallows
whistling and bending about you, to a seat on the parapet;
and behold! the long avenue lies directly below, reaching
over the high arches of the bridge at your feet, with the great
stone pillars surmounted by the cross at its centre. To the
right is a square full of stone seats and enormous old trees,
built in among the chimney tops like a hanging garden;
on the left a pathway, cobble paved, two bare walls high as
houses, and showing the tips of trees above, leads toward the
strange old tower of the cathedral. These narrow paved
ways are irresistible; you wander lingeringly up and down
on side-walks two feet wide, one foot wide, no width at all;
you see houses with wide window ledges full of flowers, and
bright faces of children peeping through; houses with windows like round loopholes; houses with mere slits in the deep
stone walls and gloomy archways, as if each were an ancient
fortress; houses with no windows at all. And everywhere
high walled gardens, giving you a hint of fragrance and
greenery behind their stone gratings, or a rabble of child
voices from the concealed playground of a school. You
burrow like a mole through half underground passages, with

only a narrow band of sky above to tell you it is brilliant daylight in the upper world, half in awe, half in fascination of the dark corners and blank walls. Then at each few moments you debouch into a dazzle of air and sunshine; and there is one of the quiet little breathing places, so profoundly silent, so glowing in light that the transition is almost painfully pleasant. Under the old trees will be one or two old, old people sunning themselves in the warmth, or a nurse with a couple of quaint, noiseless, white-capped babies, and nothing else in motion, save the wind in the tree-tops, or the swallows shrilling with whistling flight. Such a sense of perfect calm and rest as these sunny, half-suspended gardens give, I never experienced before even among mountains and deserts. For here the abodes of men, the surrounding silent, high, grave walls seem to clamour for utterance, and not be able to break the spell.

These unexpected small pleasaunces meet you in every quarter, always with flights of steps going up to or leading from them, some cut in the white rock as if you were descending a cavern, some hid in a tangle of greenery like a slender ladder of vines and flowers. There is one such beautiful dreamy spot in the terraced gardens of the Archbishop's Palace overlooking the river and valley; and a strange sundial in the silent courtyard outside with the pregnant motto, "Transit hora; manent opera; dum tempus habemus operemur bonum."

There is another facing the inner court of the Château, where the equestrian statue of Louis XII., in the arch above the main portal, blazes with gilt trappings against a background covered with the golden lilies of France. There is one at the head of the "little ladder of St. Honoré," and one at the corner of the Eastern Promenade, and one here and one there through the entire network of narrow lanes which really makes up the city. From some of these, a magnificent view of the town itself and the low-lying forest-crowned valley can be had; with the river running its swift, placid way through orchards and green meadows; from others, only the narrow dark arches and pathways leading in different directions, like so many threads from the centre of a spider's web. They are built above and below, about and between the walls and ditches which made up the ancient fortifications of the town, and it is most sincerely to be hoped they will always remain as they are at present.

The Château, built by Louis XII. and Anne of Brittany, and enlarged by Francis I., Henry III., and Catherine de Medicis, is in the strangest medley of styles. At either end, with walls nine feet thick, a massive donjon rises like a precipice, pierced only by a few narrow windows; between stretches the beautiful façade, with deep recessed arches over each window in three stories, and a light and elegant Italian loggia above, with graceful pillars of white stone rising above a beautiful balustrade of the same material. The alcoves around the recessed windows are emblazoned in blue and gold, while the outer elevation is in the same creamy stone, carved in an infinite diversity of design, with shields, mottoes, grinning gargoyles, and an intricacy of flowers and scroll-work. The fortresses have held their own against the ravages of time and the buffets of adverse fortune; the other portions have been wonderfully restored, even to the colour and style of decoration, by the Historic Society of France. No wonder they should desire to preserve a spot so rich in history. It was here Louis XII. was born, and the unhappy Claude of France, whose emblem of the swan, with an arrow piercing its breast, is to be found in some of the chambers; here Catherine de Medicis plotted her crimes and ambitions, and Henry III. convoked the Councils of State to legalise his intolerance of the Huguenots; here Marie de Medicis fled, with Armand Duplessis de

Richelieu in her train, only to find her retreat changed to
a prison, from which she escaped by a ladder of ropes and
the kindly shadow of night. Here Guise was trapped to
his death in the weak and cruel king's bedchamber, and
Catherine mixed poisons with conspiracies, and Louis XIV.
met fair La Valliere under the trees of the park. To-day
it is all renewed for modern eyes to look upon. There are
chambers and chapels and studies of the different royalties,
with their favourite devices blazoned in blue and gold over
the groined roofs; and the wonderful mantels, carved and
illuminated like ancient missals; and the alcoves above the
kneeling-chairs, rich with rare splendours of glass in the small
leaden frames. There are secret doors in the wainscoting,
which used to be hung with tapestries, and secret stairways
in the heavy walls, climbing up to the beautiful battlements,
or down to the horrors of dungeons too infernal to speak
of. There is the private cabinet of Catherine, sheathed in
carved oak, and gilded until it shines like a tapestry of
gold, with each of its 248 panels cut in a different device
as fine and delicate as lace-work. You may be sure there
were secret places there, and plenty of them. And there
are private chapels and cloistered arches, and the great
Hall of Fêtes, which witnessed the assemblage of the States
General in 1588, and what must be one of the most beautiful bits of architecture of the Renaissance left to the world
—a staircase of carved greystone, built in a succession
of open pillared colonnades, carved, of extreme elegance.
With its wonderful heights and dimensions, and its richness of colour, this chateau gives one a new idea of the
luxury of those early centuries we are wont to term and to
fancy barbaric. Under these lofty ceilings and columned
galleries, between soft tapestries and rugs, with walls nine
feet deep, and endless entourage of fawning courtiers,
what could kings and queens know of the common rabble

who lived almost like wild beasts in the huts outside their gates?

But we are staying too long at the château. For there are yet the pretty open markets to be spoken of, and the ancient fountain of Louis XII., and the monumental staircase, with its bronze statue of Denis Papinaton, and the Hotel d'Alluye, with its gallery ornamented with medallions in terra cotta of the eleven Cæsars. And then the college, the seminary, the Bishop's Palace, the old cemetery, the Beauvoir Tower, the Palace of Justice, and the Château of St. Lazare, where Victor Hugo lived in 1820. Not to speak of Chambord, that "Pearl of Renaissance," which would require a letter for itself, but which in spite of all its splendour is more memorable to us in that Molière gave here his first representation of Pourceaugnac, and Le Bourgeois Gentilhomme. Ah! Blois! Blois! How many of your glories your poor chronicler has left unhonoured and unsung in spite of all the delight you have given her! One thing, however, shall not go without mention—the Crème de Saint Gervais! Think of cream in a little brown earthen pot, tied up in vine leaves, so thick that you have to scoop it out like butter. And of a fragrance! Think then of strawberries as big as your two thumbs, dipped, rolled into this delicious bath, and eaten in a blanket of powdered sugar. Think of this twice every day for breakfast and for dinner, with some eight or nine courses preceding, one of which shall be a species of bouchées of truffled unknown delicacies, and another a ragout of duck with mushrooms. And think that with a pretty room, with a shaded balcony all to yourself, and a landlady who gives you a smile and a bunch of roses every morning, in the best hotel in town, you pay only two dollars a day. Then don't think any more, but say with me from the bottom of your hearts, "Ah! Blois! Blois!"

CHAPTER XVI.

TOURS.

THE country between Blois and Tours at midsummer can only be described as a garden; every foot of it shows such marks of careful cultivation, and it is such a wilderness of flowers. The railroad is bordered mainly with acacias now in full blossom, so that the air is as if blown through an orange grove. Wheat-fields are so sown with poppies that they look more like beds of flowers than of grain; the second crop of peas is full of pale, delicate clusters; the barley shines like sheafs of silver through its long, silky beard; strawberries glow like rose-beds; the banks of the river and hedges of the roads are covered with wild bluebells and tall yellow fleur de lis. Even the vineyards look like plantations of young shrubbery, and the beautiful grouping of trees scattered here and there over the wide plain make it appear as a gentleman's park might that is under constant surveillance. It is so wonderful to see this unending beauty, which care and industry have created, that one never ceases admiring. There are no stones, no rough spots, no waste places. Everything is finished to the last degree of perfection.

Tours is larger and richer and finer, perhaps I might even say more beautiful, than Blois; but it is not half so fascinating. Tours is a provincial demoiselle, very chic, very well dressed, with a good dowry to support her pretensions; but just a trifle too self-possessed and gaily-dressed. You see all my lady's airs and graces at once, and it pleases you to flirt a while. But Blois is one of those demure, long-lashed, dark-eyed little creatures whom you do not notice in the beginning, but who suddenly one day looks up with an arch sparkle, and shows her small white teeth in a dazzle of a smile that changes all her face into a sort of dark splendour, and there you are, made captive heart and soul; you don't know how, to you don't know what. It is the simplest thing in the world, however. You have fallen in love. But we will not grow sentimental. Tours is very well when you cannot help yourself.

It has a great deal to be honestly proud of. There is a magnificent promenade under quadruple rows of fine trees, running, or rather walking, for a mile through the centre of its principal boulevards. There is one of the largest printing and publishing houses in France, employing 1200 men; that of Mame, which occupies commodious and handsome quarters. There is a cathedral which is finest of all in the valley of the Loire, and second only in magnificence to the four great piles of Amiens, Chartres, Rheims, and Bourges. It still preserves in the choir some of the most remarkable windows in existence, dating from the thirteenth century, and priceless as specimens of the work in glass of that period. There is the Tower of Charlemagne, which that monarch raised over the remains of his wife Luitgarde, as the Eastern Prince made the Taj Mahul the shrine of his beloved. Only since Luitgarde was a third wife, and I think there was a fourth before the connubial chapter ended, so the Frankish monument is not quite so beautiful as the Persian. Then there are churches without number, each remarkable in some particular way—one for its pictures, one for its age, one for its riches, one for its architect. There are two which deserve better uses, turned now into shops for produce and grain; and a little chapel of the twelfth century which is a real curiosity in architecture. Besides, one is constantly coming across fine buildings, the remains, in more or less perfect preservation, of old convents and cloisters; some still retained for religious uses, and some devoted to the more modern god of trade. There is a theatre, all new and spic and span, with sculptured façade and Corinthian columns, and statues and masks and what-not, in the approved hodge-podge style, which is to art what opera bouffe is to music. And there are really fine markets, and a handsome fountain, and houses with traditions of all sorts of famous occupants, from Tristan l'Hermite to Mlle. de la Valliere—which is certainly a sufficiently wide difference.

Along with all these, Tours has a pedigree as long as my arm, of Saints and Sinners, each sufficiently remarkable in his or her way to merit a capital letter in designating them. Besides St. Martin, who was brought here after his death, there is St. Perpet, who was his successor as bishop; and St. Gregoire, who wrote the first history of France somewhere about the beginning of the seventh century. There was also Alcuin, the Abbot of St. Martin's, who ought certainly to be canonised, although he isn't, for having opened here the first public school of theology and philosophy in France; and sweet St. Clothilde, who died here. Heading the other list comes Louis XI., a mad demon clothed in the mantle of religion, who paid the city the poor compliment of making it the seat of his favourite residence of Plessis-les-Tours, where he and his honest friend Olivier, the barber, could hang men from limbs of trees and snare them in iron cages. But since the devil is never so black as he is painted, this same royal madman helped to make the place of his preference great and rich. He established manufactories of silk, and cloth of gold and silver, and offered such advantages and privileges to workmen and merchants that the population increased enormously. But the chronology of vice is not interesting. Since we have found that a good word can be said about Louis, let us hope the same would be true of the

I

wickedness which would follow him as leader, and leave it in peace.

If Tours, however, had no argument in its favour than that it is the gateway to so many of the historic properties of France, it would have its excuse for being. Loches is within an hour of it, and Montbazm and Couzieres; so are Cinq Mars and Chateau Renault and Langeais. So is Chenonçeaux, most strangely beautiful of all this bevy of beauties. The chateau, built on a series of arches which entirely cross the Cher—built, in reality, upon a great bridge of stone—is unique in this regard, as well as in the romance and variety of its historic reminiscence. It was here that Henry II. installed Diana of Poitiers with the title of Duchess of Valentinois. When the death of the king put a period to the wicked beauty's plans of limitless expenditure, she exchanged with Catherine de Medicis her royal lover's gift for Chaumont, which was already finished, while Chenonçeaux was not well begun. Catherine immediately proceeded to enrich and beautify this, which became her favourite residence, and from that time to this it has been in hands which were able and willing to preserve its rare charms. Strange to say, it was in the hands of a commoner, M. Dupin, that it attained its greatest brilliancy. During the sixty or seventy years of the ownership of this family, it received as guests all that was most notable and worthy in French society; and even the Revolution, when it came, spared the house as well as the owners, who had learned to make themselves beloved as well as honoured. Buffon was received here, and Montesquieu, Condellac, Bolingbroke, and Voltaire. Rousseau spent some years superintending the education of the heir of the house and writing verses, "which," he says, "had no other virtue than being funny." One can imagine the superb company in the superb palace, or wandering about the grounds; through the terraced garden of the dead and gone Diana, beautiful still with her flowers and fountains; through the bright alleys of the park, and the stately glories of the long galleries which Catherine had built above the river arches. Imagination cannot picture anything so lovely as this mass of towers and spires in carved greystone, with the long span of the galleries, which rise for three stories behind, all lifted upon the beautiful arches through which the beautiful river flows so swiftly. Inside the first portcullis—for one only enters this enchanting spot by crossing two drawbridges—a donjon tower of the fifteenth century guards the approach to the portal of the chateau. Within the noble rooms, with high ceilings of carved oak, chimney pieces fifteen feet high, and blazoned in blue and gold, doors and window screens that are masses of open work, as fine and delicate as old lace, and royal ciphers wrought between fleur de lis and laurel wreaths, make an ensemble of magnificent decoration. The most charming nooks for boudoirs open from each great salon or chamber into the round towers. They told us fairy stories of the manner in which these walls and floors had been furnished by the last owner, Madame Pelouse, the sister of the whilom notorious M. Wilson, whose name figured so unpleasantly during the last part of his father-in-law, President Grevy's, administration. Hung from ceiling to floor with rose-coloured silks and rare tapestries, filled with statues and priceless bric-a-brac, adorned with every elegance that limitless wealth and taste could devise, it must have been a dream of beauty. In the long Salon des Fêtes the walls were still covered with fine old paintings, some sacred, some exceedingly profane— as one of Gabrielle, mistress of Henry, and her two sisters, taken as the Three Graces. A portrait of Madame Pelouse, by Carolus Duran, of more than life-size, and occupying the place of honour, shows her a coarse, but fine-looking woman, with a suspicion of beard on the chin, and the pose of an empress. Fortunately beards do not interfere with poses.

That was all that was left now of the career of folly which, in twenty-four years, had reached the end of the endless riches. "But Madame will understand the money was thrown away by handfuls. There were fortunes spent on the chateau, and fortunes on the grounds, and fortunes on the fêtes. It was a river of money, and there were so many to drink it." The concierge's metaphor was mixed, but it was explicit. Madame Pelouse is in Paris, and beautiful Chenonçeaux is at Blirè, in the hands of the Credit Foncier of France. So its wheel of fortune is ready for another turn.

It would be hard to say, though, that Chenonçeaux the chateau is any more lovely than Chenonçeaux the hamlet. Such a nest of verdure and flowers under the poplar trees. Such dear, quaint, dark little houses, each with its garden behind it, and its wooden shuttered windows turned blankly to the village street. Such views up and down the shady lanes, with the quiet Cher flowing through the quiet landscape. And such a delicious small inn, with the daintiest small parlour, hung about the walls with blue and gold faience of Turenne, and radiant with great masses of flowers, in which one can have such an excellent dinner. Your strawberries will be brought in from the garden while your omelette and chop disappear, and there is clotted cream as rich as that of St. Gervais, of blessed memory. "Madame is regarding the flowers! But yes, they are really very fine. They are the work of the grandfather, who has spent all his life in cultivating the peony. And it is just at this moment that his grandson, my brother, has taken the first prize for the tree peonies at the great Paris Exposition of flowers. But yes, it is an honour surely. And the grandfather is well pleased. Perhaps Madame might like to see the garden?" And the pretty little maid of the inn, who is doing the honours of the strawberries and cream, takes Madame, who certainly does like to see, through a grilled gate into a wilderness of strange peonies, but sublimated into sizes and colours and rare pale tints, flames of fire, masses of snow, wonderful balls of amber, of rose, of exquisite gradations that no harsh known name will fit, large and rich as those famous growths of Southern California, and filling the space between the grey walls with an unspeakable luxury. Fragrant, too, so that the last charm is added to their beauty. No wonder they took the first prize at Paris. Here in the midst sits the old grandfather, clear of eye and bright of cheek yet, after the sunshine of nearly eighty summers. Each flower that he has loved and tended bears the name of one of the family. "Regard how we are all here, Madame. Here is the mother, that large red one; and here my sister Réné; and here the brother Pierre, who is now in Paris; and there the cousins; and there the aunt. There is the grandfather himself, with grandmere near him. It is a real *fête de famille.* And mine? Over there in the corner with the little golden heart." Something else besides the flower has a golden heart, little maid, if that is any better than the ordinary one of flesh and blood. May it long remain untarnished. And may more of the world that is looking in its haphazard way for rest and refreshment go down to find both at the "Inn of the Good Labourer," under the poplars of Chenonçeaux.

We have been struck all through this journey with the wonderful care taken to prevent railroad accidents in France. No one is allowed on any account to walk on the rails, and a prohibition here means something. In the stations there is one side absolutely for arrival and one for departure, so that the two can never clash; and one can only cross the track at a special spot under the surveillance of a watchful guardian. No matter where or how often country roads are intersected by the railway, they either pass under or over; or if by chance they cross on the same level, there are two gates always kept shut, with a cottage near by in which the flagman lives who opens the way to the passer-by. A foot passenger can open for himself, but there are invariably the two closed gates to open. When one thinks of the recklessness with which the roads and streets outside our American cities, indeed, often within them, run across the railroads, and the number of casualties resulting, one is filled with admiration at this constant exact watchfulness. No wonder the people pride themselves on few accidents.

SWITZERLAND.

CHAPTER XVII.

NEUCHÂTEL.

WHEN the tower has for months been the loftiest thing in the field of vision, and you close your eyes in its shadow some evening in a " waggon-lit " or sleeping-car, it is sufficiently startling to open them next morning among the gorges of the Jura Mountains leading into Neuchâtel. The change is so pronounced—you have forgotten so utterly amid those fair, fertile, boundless plains of France, that there are any mountainous countries—that the sensation is startling. These about you are not very lofty; the train winds in and out half way up a thousand foot slope, sheer precipitous height on one side, deep valleys full of cultivated fields on the other. The little hamlets and isolated houses are of a new order. The roofs are dark brown instead of red, and they slope with broad eaves to within ten feet of the ground. The single clear story is packed with windows, wider than they are long; a single house has as many as a French village. Sometimes the wooden beams under the eaves are gaily coloured; often there are carvings on window-frames and lintels. These pretty picturesque dwellings are contrasted with others high and narrow, having three or four stories below, and one or two others in the sharp gables. There are pastures among the thick pine woods on the hillsides, so steep that one would think flocks and herds must be spiked into the earth to prevent their tumbling over into the gardens beneath. There is a rapid-rushing, broad stream, pushing so swiftly through the valley that it is a white foam of rapids, and hurling itself against the rocky sides with such fury that it is dissipated into smoke. And every moment some sudden, swift turn of the road bears one into new regions of beauty. The mountain mists are already lifted from the lowlands, but still hide the craggy points above; sometimes a rocky formation like a battlement crowns a sturdy peak; once an old castle-like chateau shows upon a height; the air is full of the strong sweet spiciness of pine boughs. By-and-by a final curve brings one into sight of a mirror-like smoothness of blue water shining in the morning; beyond it rises a billowy expanse of mountains—real mountains—lifting and losing themselves amid the upper clouds. If you were being led unknowingly without any premonition of destination, your heart would tell you it was Switzerland.

Is every town and village in this wonderful world born to a divine dower of beauty? Here is this little spot, rising in irregular terraces above the lake, with the Alps set in shining panorama before it, and its quaint medley of modern French and old-time houses. The streets run principally on lines parallel with the water, connected by short steep passages or flights of steps. They are so quiet, so very quiet, that the occasional carts and omnibuses must herald their rare appearance with great salvos of whip-cracking; and the houses are all furnished with tin ear-trumpets in the roof to help them catch the faint sounds of life below. At least I do not know what else the queer little excrescences can be, or what they are meant for. There are pretty chateaux by the water-side surrounded by gardens; and fountains everywhere, flowing from bases of pillared statues into circular stone basins, wherein good Haus-Fraus come to wash their clothes in big tubs, with a piece of smooth plank for a washboard. There is a little church of the twelfth century with a modern Gothic cloister, on a terrace far above the roofs of the lower town, opening on a garden with an ivy-covered battlemented wall that is simply delicious. Through the embrasures one looks across at the Alps, snow-crowned from Pilatus to Mont Blanc—a dream of delight if the coy creatures ever show themselves, which they did not do through the four too short days of our stay. They must condescend sometimes, however, for I have one of the loveliest photographs in the world which shows a long line of radiant peaks melting into a cloudless sky. Even when half invisible, they are beautiful enough to stir one's pulses with that ineffable lonesome happiness which only mountains can give.

There are delightful excursions to be made by diligence, carriage, or the busy little dark steamers which float like black swans up and down the lake. Chaumont gives, when it chooses, a marvellous view of the lake of Neuchâtel, and that of Bienne to the north-east, with its far-away chain of peaks. The railroad over Les Hauts-Geneveys brings you to a point where half an hour's climb shows Mont Blanc in all its splendour, filling the extreme point of the southern horizon. Farther on, the queer little town of Chaux de Fonds, in a valley which seems lifted away from the rest of the world, is a vast manufactory of watches. One enters upon it through labyrinths of tunnels, to find a conglomerate of little workshops, wherein every creature belonging to the place is fitting cog-wheels, coiling springs and adjusting regulators. Instead of being born with a silver spoon in his mouth, the lucky Chaux-de-Fondser comes into the world with a silver watch in his pocket. Timepieces are so cheap that children could buy them instead of bons-bons. Locle, farther on, is a prettier spot given to the same traffic, and with two side issues in the Saut-du-Doubs, a pretty waterfall dashing between extremely sharp cliffs nearly five hundred feet high, and the long narrow lake of Brenets, whose deep green waters stretch through a gorge of splintered rock at its outlet. The colour is like the wonderful green of the Merced River in the Yosemite.

We were for a long time puzzled to know how horses and carriages got over the steep grades which separate the main streets. It looked as if they must be helped from one level to another with derricks, or lowered on toboggan slides; no right-minded quadruped, except a goat, could ever allow himself to be cajoled into any of these ladder-like cross-cuts. If there were more horses in the town, one could fancy a special group for every terrace; but there were too few for any such hypothesis. After the omnipresence of the Parisian coachman and his animal, it is a relief to be able to count on your fingers all that could be met in a mid-day walk. For one waggon of milk or bread or vegetables drawn in the usual way, there are ten pulled along by bloused men or aproned women. Even the postman pushes a little two-wheeled cart before him on his daily rounds. Life is so peaceful, so unhurried, that they probably see no reason for rushing through it on horseback instead of afoot.

Yet it has its little bustle here too. At noon and night, when the children and workpeople are returning home, there is quite a fine hubbub of laughter and voices, and hob-nailed shoes. In the evening this almost becomes noise. Young men go by singing two or three part choruses with loud lusty voices; the children chatter and shriek like so many magpies; the postillions driving from the late trains to the Hotel du Faucon or the Grand Hotel du Lac crack their whips like a regiment of Cossacks. The town-crier walks briskly down a side street, and after a rataplan upon the drum announces a sale to-morrow, or an auction, or a lost child, or a coming circus, and with another rataplan marches off again. Mothers from upper windows exchange confidences with other mothers on the side-walk, both meanwhile knitting on the long white stockings which are here part of every good woman's birthright—and very good legs they have to fill them. Swallows in dark flights go twittering shrilly about the tall roofs; the heavy wooden shutters are thrown back to let the houses open their eyes a little; the green waters of the lake are gay with pleasure-boats, and the broad promenade on its borders is full of easy-going idlers after the busy hours of the day. But, as in Jean Ingelow's verse, all these sounds and sights—

"Like ringdoves, make not quiet less."

It is still as reposeful as if every one were in bed and asleep.

To all English-speaking people, but more especially to Americans, the little town will always have an added interest from the fact that so many of its folk are—

"Bons Amis
De Jean Louis Agassiz;"

and that it was here the beloved and brilliant naturalist spent his novitiate in the order of science. The first fourteen years of his professional work were passed as lecturer in one of the departments of the College; and it was during this time that his observations among the great glaciers of the neighbourhood began to make his attainments known to the scientific world. There is still preserved the valuable cabinet of Natural History, collected by him during his connection with the institution; and many an incident is yet fresh in the popular memory, which would prove the same devotion to science that caused him afterwards to decline a lucrative engagement on the plea that he "could not afford to make money."

Let me remark, *en passant*, that if you have any desire to be a little ill, as a sort of experiment, there is no better place than Neuchâtel. You can have the sympathy of a most kindly landlord, and a good bed in a good room, looking out upon a sunny courtyard, with a fountain in the centre, where splashing of water among the goldfishes, and the singing of birds among flowers, shall be the only sounds to hear. And you can have a physician whose clear keen eyes and cheering smile will do you as much good as his medicines, which are infallible. What a pity that it is wrong to be personal; and that I cannot therefore tell you that the room is to be found in the clean small Hotel du Faucon, and the good Samaritan in Dr. Ernest de Reynier. For to a stranger in a strange land, these little items might sometimes be of interest.

. . . .

We found before leaving Neuchâtel how the horses actually came down from the hilltops. They are harnessed to waggons, pieces of plain board are fastened under the wheels, and the dead weight of the loaded cart keeps the animal from turning double somersaults into the valley. Be it understood, however, that this is only possible on some of the graded roads, not the steep ones. It is yet a profound mystery how they are ever hauled back again.

CHAPTER XVIII.

BERNE.

AT every mile of the way as one dips into Switzerland, the surroundings become more and more picturesque. The great roofs of the houses grow larger and darker; outside galleries creep under the eaves with clumsy stairways leading to them; stables for cattle and living rooms for their owners are enclosed within the same four walls. Vineyards planted on narrow terraces raised over stone embankments run up the steep slopes of the hills to the rocky buttresses above, from which the mountains spring into the upper air. Small fields of grain, and bits of pasture, fill every gap between the lowland forests of pine and fir. In the sheltered valleys, wheat of an unusual height grows yellow in the sun, with blue cornflowers fringing the edges. In the house-gardens among the hamlets there are everywhere masses of white and red roses, trimmed like trees into one straight bare stem, with a luxuriant richness of bloom on top. The mountain streams dash themselves down precipitous rocky channels in a torrent of liquid malachite with deep emerald streaks against the white foam. Now and again a tiny lake lies darkly shining in shadow of the cliffs, or a gorge like some of the Colorado cañons gives back the roar of the flying train in thunderous echoes. Everywhere there are tunnels which toss one like a shuttlecock out of light into darkness, and from darkness back to light again. And constantly the glimpses of distant peaks behind the veiling of cloud which shrouds their brows, become more and more majestic.

In the fields and valleys, as in France, the women and men work side by side. Digging with long spades, weeding, haymaking, binding the vines to their trellises on the rocky slopes, there is no material difference, save that of dress, to show that they are of another calibre. They are as brown as the men, and as large, and as lusty, and as ugly. As ugly? They are uglier. Only for a certain comeliness in the female face and form which is never exacted from the male, at least of the human species. But these large-boned, swarth-browed, too often bearded amazons, who stride over the ploughed land like troopers, and leap a four or five foot stream like springboks, have lost whatever traditions of grace belong to the sex. Of course there are exceptions; and at a distance, in the holiday dress of the different cantons, like this of Berne, with its white chemisette, black velvet bodice, and silver chains, they are really pretty to look at. But do not push curiosity too closely.

Berne is always interesting. The novelty of construction in the queer old houses, the wide smiling beauty of the modern boulevards and squares, and the wonderful curve of the river, which almost forms an island of the peninsula upon which the town is built, make one's heart glad at the first glance. Something of solidity and strength in the aspect of the place and people recalls involuntarily the history of its old renown in arms, when under Rudolph Erlach and other valiant leaders it repulsed every effort to rob it of freedom, and remained independent in the midst of feudalism. Like most Swiss towns, it is built on an upper and lower level; the one with its streets, houses, and river running in part entirely under the bridges of the other. It is beautifully quaint and irregular. All the streets are simply wide-paved roadways, with a swift current from the Aar running through a shallow canal, either open or covered, in the centre; and spouting at every hundred feet into the round stone basin of a fountain from pipes at the foot of a statue-crowned figure. About these fountains the washing and cleaning of the city go on from Monday morning to Saturday night. The lower floors of the substantial four-story houses open directly from the roadway in large round arches, immensely heavy and low, under which the side-walks run in a series of arcades. The shops, which almost invariably take up the ground floors, are as dark as a pocket, but the people are so honest that you might buy with your eyes shut. Here and there, these cool, dim cloisters of side-walks go up a few steps, or down; twist suddenly ten feet to the right, or ten feet to the left; grow wide, grow narrow, or stop altogether. Never being able to see where you are going for more than a few rods, you blunder toward your destination or away from it, as fortune is kind or fickle. Nor is the middle of the carriage-road a much safer guide. Sometimes in mid-career it runs plump against some remnant of the Middle Ages in the shape of a clock-tower or the massive buttress of some ancient dwelling. Part of the thoroughfare will flow on through the archway which usually pierces this picturesque obstruction; part will turn the corner and meander off on the other side; part will lose itself wholly, never to be found again. You pick up the thread of your wanderings as you may, and journey on. There can never be too many of these irregularities, for each is a delight in this straight, conventional, commonplace world. As for roofs and chimneys, there can be nothing so rich as Berne. The eaves project ten or twelve feet in huge balconies, curved slightly on the edges like Chinese pagodas; the chimneys rise in greyish-white stacks from the dull red tiles, high and low, pointed like steeples, gabled like house-tops, carved, curved, plain, in a forest of grotesque forms. The sameness which the unbroken lines of the façades upon the street would naturally give without any relief from side-walk or trees, is modified by these outlines into something rich and attractive.

K

Outside every window is a small iron railing, which forms a back to the window-seat within. These are decorated with flowers, with scarlet cushions, and with bright ornaments, so that the effect is full of animation. Under the side-walk arches are broad seats of stone and wood, where sometimes goods are displayed, but oftenest the busy Haus-Frau sits pulling wool, making mattresses, or knitting. Such a world of knitters! Walking the streets, gossiping with the neighbours, watching the children, rocking the cradle, the Bernese woman knits, knits, knits, like the Tricoteuses of the French Revolution. Only there are no tragedies woven into these stockings. For amusement's sake, we once counted the number of people in the little park by the cathedral on a warm June afternoon. Out of a hundred and nineteen, a hundred and nine were knitting like machines, and four of the remaining ten were tourists.

We shall always remember Berne with love and gratitude, because it gave us the first glimpse of the real glory of Switzerland. We had been wandering all day from the Bear Pits to the Federal Palace, among the wonderful old wood carvings of the Cathedral, and along the fine promenade of the Little Rampart. Tired of novelties, we were sitting down to rest on the river-bank, where the beautiful lofty arches of the New Bridge span the rushing torrent by a bound of a hundred feet into the air. Just below, the broad ferry-boat, swinging at the end of its long chain, crossed backward and forward with its load of town and peasant folk, the brown young ferryman steering with his hand on the long tiller astern. Far up and down the steep banks, lovely fields and drooping acacias hung above the green water, and surrounded the pretty chalet-like houses, as if to prevent their toppling into the stream. The sky above was glowing with intense summer heat, only tempered by the refreshing air blowing from the heights across the river, while a thick grey cloud covered the horizon. Suddenly this lifted, like a curtain;

and there, set in an arch of brilliant azure, were three peaks of the Alps, radiant, pure, shining, more white than the clouds above them, more dazzling than any other enchantment God has given to man on earth. They shone in a cleft between two dark heights, sombre and fir-crowned, and one could no more look upon their glory than upon the sun at noonday. In whatever part of the world these transcendent witnesses of the majesty of the Creator rise, they usurp the soul to the exclusion of every other emotion. One feels no longer heat or cold, loneliness or companionship; something divine and sustaining takes hold of the immortal in us; and in the glow and greatness of the impulse which sways us, we are conscious of having been made in His image and likeness. The vision lasted not long, and faded again beneath a down-dropping cloud as swiftly as it had appeared. But the spot which held it for those few breathless minutes will always have its especial place in remembrance.

It was at Berne, too, that we first saw a sight which we found often repeated afterward in many Swiss towns, the harnessing of a dog and a man, or a dog and a woman, between the shafts of small waggons, instead of the more costly horse. The dog always seemed to enjoy his position and make sport of it; it would be untrue to say as much for the two-footed animal beside him; yet the faces as a rule are so expressionless, that it would be hard to judge. At least if there is little enthusiasm here, there is less discontent. And how the two yoked creatures, with their high-piled load of fagots or vegetables, would run over the roughly paved streets, as if they were smoothest asphalt pavements! It was as if there were no such attributes as tired backs and aching arms known to human nature. I wonder if some such heroic measure would remove them from our side of the water. Or would this Swiss movement cure need Swiss muscles to work upon?

The old fathers of the town must have been a jolly set of burghers, with a turn for practical jokes. Instead of the graceful forms, classic or romantic, with which other cities ornament their fountains, those light-hearted patriarchs chose new models. They preferred the ridiculous rather than the sublime; so through all the town, in street and market-place, we have the fantastic instead of the sentimental. Here is the Pied Piper, with his baby train pressing after in hot haste. Here is the Ogre Croquemitaine, with one child half down his capacious throat, and his pockets bulging with a dozen others who are to complete his tender meal. Here is the Great Bear in full panoply of helmet, shield, and spear, ready to protect the burg of his adoption. Here are Archers and Lion-tamers, Griffins and Hobgoblins, with every shape of grinning gargoyle from which water can be poured. They all seem in place here in those quaint, long, twisted thoroughfares, with the red-cushioned window-ledges brightening the old grey houses, and the dark side-walks hidden behind their thick stone arches as if they had retired to sleep. The figure of the Bear, from which Berne takes its name, is blended in every conceivable way with its art and architecture. It is as omnipresent as Joan of Arc at Orleans, or the Wolf in ancient Rome. It is carved in wood, moulded in bronze, modelled in marble, baked in gingerbread, boiled in candy. A favourite toy is a bear fulfilling some of the functions of human beings; painting at an easel, teaching school, sweeping floors, hammering shoes; and the popular bon-bon is a white sugar bear with a red peppermint tongue, furiously dashing across a chocolate field. The eyes of little children follow this coveted tit-bit with awe and longing, while even the elders regard it with proud complacency.

CHAPTER XIX.

INTERLAKEN.

WHEN the debt of gratitude the world owes to the monks of the Middle Ages is finally acknowledged, there will be found in it few items of more importance to the happiness and elevation of mankind than that work of the Augustinians, who accomplished the task of creating a little foothold of land between the lakes of Thun and Brienz, about the beginning of the thirteenth century. To have left Interlaken as a heritage to mankind is to have merited the blessing of posterity for ever. "The Lovely Little Plain," as the common folk who came after the monks were dead and gone christened it, is so very lovely. Set between two steep spurs of mountain chains, which rise in rugged precipices and overhanging pine forests in almost perpendicular heights above the valley, it looks through the dark gorge of the Lauterbrunnen straight upon the dazzling beauty of that Virgin of the Alps, the Jungfrau. The rich soil, which has been washed for centuries down the slopes by winter storm and spring freshet, sustains a luxuriance of vegetation almost tropical in its variety and strength. Every house nestles in a wilderness of roses and vines; the hedges are masses of flowers; the streets arches of overhanging boughs, which frame the wild grandeur of more distant views. The exquisite country roads wind through fields of wheat taller than one's head, through small market gardens as attractive as pleasure grounds, through pastures sweet with the breath of newly-mown hay, with always before, behind, above, the glory of the mountains. The swift, narrow river runs in curves below its rustic bridges at the very foot of the Harderwand, and in every direction forest paths lead toward marvellous views from seemingly inaccessible points.

How differently one understands Auerbach's "On the Heights" after seeing one such Alpine village. Yonder, high up—so high that it looks as if only the flight of a bird could ever reach, or the foot of a bird ever rest upon it—is a farmhouse, with its fields stretching up the perpendicular rifts in the side of the precipice, fastened by some marvel of gravitation on that airy plateau. With the glass you will see that many of its acres are planted between rows of stakes driven in parallel lines, to keep the upper levels from falling in a landslide upon the lower. You will see, too, the slow moving forms of cows and sheep no larger than stones grazing behind the low stone walls, which serve as barricades between them and destruction. What repose, what isolation must be the lot of those who look from that dizzy eminence down upon the valley below. What silent sobriety of thought, what close intimacy with the moods of nature, that lonely, breezy atmosphere must bring to those who breathe it. And what supernal beauty of outlook to feed upon. How could one bred in that pure, free space, like an eagle's eyrie, ever be satisfied with the noise and dust of this busy scene below.

Meantime the busy scene below is very charming for those who have not been born with the instincts of a chamois. There is the Hoheweg, passing first between its little and big chalets, with the most entrancing small shops on the ground floor, and overhead, under the big eaves, such quaint carved galleries of wood, and little windows, with diamond panes, as one has been used to see in Swiss carvings. Some of the fronts are queerly etched in figures of birds and beasts, or engraved with maxims and proverbs in large German text. Some are intricately adorned with open-work scrolls, cut by hand in the long winter evenings. All have their window-sills full of flowering plants, and their porches shaded with vines. Sometimes a stiff little garden, with the bushes cut into unnatural shapes, or trained after unusual fashions, is at the front or side. Sometimes the door is below, and sometimes again above the narrow side path. There is a constant going and coming of vehicles, from the big diligence of the hotels to the small donkey cart of the peasants. You meet countrymen with a bunch of Edelweiss or pine-needles in the band of their felt hats; peasant girls in the pretty costume of the Bernese cantons; town folk with their heavy hobnailed shoes and thick woollen dresses; and strangers from all parts of the world. It is a perfect Babel of tongues and temperaments. Everybody seems to speak at least two—French with some other language as a patois—except the English, who deliver themselves in their several dialects, with such wonderful alternations of broadness and flatness in pronunciation, as it is rarely given one to hearken to. If there is any rule at all to regulate the sounds of vowels and consonants in Anglo-Saxon, the average British tourist should be arraigned before some moral court of justice for the crime of *lèse majesté*. One's ear has to be cultivated as carefully to discover the meaning of their unknown tongue as to translate any of the foreign idioms. Whatever dreadful arrogance of custom or straining after effect has produced this result it would be impossible to determine; but certain I am that Dan Chaucer to-day would be quite as intelligible to the majority of his hearers as his degenerate descendant.

But to return to the Höheweg, or the Main street, if you prefer it that way. Soon it broadens into the centre of a half-mile open space; a wide lawn and park on one side, extending to the nearer mountains, the Breitlauenen and

Suleck; a line of goodly hotels on the other, gay with every form of modern prettiness, balconies, and towers, and gardens full of bloom and fragrance. Thick hedges of shrubbery inside wrought iron railings separate them from the street, and give a coquettish air of seclusion; the garden paths wind between fountains and arches; the warm, soft air is deliciously fresh and sweet with odours. Everywhere still a world of people, in windows, on piazzas, walking, driving, lounging under the trees, but always with eyes turned toward the deep gorge between the hills, within which shines the Jungfrau. This is the pivot around which the whole of Interlaken revolves. Every house front turns to it, every window faces it, every path and lane leads to some turn from which a fresh beauty may be discovered in it. And no wonder, for it would be hard to conceive a fairer sight. The majestic irregularity of its outline; the sharp line of black precipice which divides its two great plateaux, and the glory of its wonderful summit shining under its eternal crown of snow, lifted like a radiant cloud above the world, make it an endless joy to look upon. The exquisite beauty of this smiling valley, which forms the foreground of the picture, intensifies its lofty silence, and makes its impressiveness a thousand-fold more marked than if it arose from a scene of desolation. This is in truth one of the secrets of the enchantment of all Swiss landscapes. The valleys are everywhere nests of loveliness, with a beauty of fitness greater than any to which mere art could ever attain; and the sombre grandeur of the mountains rises from them with an effect which of themselves alone they could never attain.

With a vision like this before one's eyes, alas! how hard it is to keep to the main street, even when there is a casino upon it lower down, full of arcades and pavilions, with reading rooms and dancing halls, spacious terraces and verandahs, with lanes and shady alleys fit for lovers' promenades. When it has an orchestra besides, which gives three concerts a day: one in the morning from 7 to 8, while the interesting invalids of the Kursaal take their wholesome potions of goat's milk whey; one from 2 to 4, while the little children and giddy youth dance upon the sward and platforms about the band stand; one from 8 to 10 in the evening, when their gracious mightinesses, the guests of the different hotels, in all the undress of evening toilette, languidly drink the strains with bumpers of beer and bottles of red wine at the same time. And it is wonderful how much, in spite of their languor, their gracious mightinesses can drink in the course of an evening. Farther on yet there are more gardens, more hotels, more parks; and at last in a green corner by itself the old whitewashed convent, delivered over now to the uses of earth instead of those of heaven. The quaint old church beside it, with its weather-beaten bell tower and spire like an extinguisher, is interesting for other reasons than even its great age. The tower rises in the centre of one side, a lofty choir and lower nave stretching from it north and south. Two doors open side by side at the top of the rude flight of steps which leads to it. One gives access to the Anglican church, which holds its services in the choir; the other to the Roman Catholic chapel, which celebrates mass in the nave. On the other side, two similar doors give entrance to the French Protestants and the Scottish Reformers respectively, while a Russian place of worship is in process of construction close by. So that four, one may say five, different religious congregations worship, each according to its lights, under what may be called the same roof. If there is as much Christian charity in the hearts of the people, Interlaken is indeed to be envied.

Like many of our own mountain towns, this one main street forms almost the entire village. One or two side lanes leading off to different hamlets east and west, and a few scattered farmhouses or pensions, make up the whole. It is not in this respect unlike Bethlehem or Jefferson in the White Mountains, or little Manitou in the shadow of Pike's Peak. What want then is congenital in the American nature, of what fair grace of imagination or artistic impulse has it been shorn, that make the results springing from these similar conditions so opposite? Bethlehem is as commonplace in its ugliness, aside from its beautiful situation, as any collection of comfortable dwellings can possibly be. Its broad side-walk, and long plain street, and dreadful square houses, large and small, all freshly painted, all uncompromisingly respectable, are detestable. There is an air of living on parade about it that knocks one's sensitive nerves as much out of tune as striking one's "funny bone." There is no softness, no sweetness, no ideality about any portion of the impression it makes upon a stranger. Yet it has had every advantage that greater opportunity, wider knowledge, and more wealth could give over this people. The proprietors of its hotels have been in a position to know what art has done in other places; the inhabitants of its cottages have spent money enough to make their homes attractive instead of repellent. What is wrong? There is not a poor shed in this valley which has not an art value, and which is not soothing to every cultivated sense. Their soft tints blend with the masses of clinging greenery about them; their shelving gables and wooden balconies—no matter how rude—their massive eaves and sweeping dark roofs, and timbered walls, are full of a refinement which is meat and drink to the imagination. And there cannot be proper spiritual health where this element of the imagination is so wholly neglected as with us. Worldly possessions and material progress are good things, but they can only become great when they are vitalised by some element of higher intelligence. What sort of civilisation is that which accepts Queen Anne cottages with impossible zigzags and useless corner fireplaces as the highest expression of fitness and elegance it has yet acquired? One little village like this of Interlaken, put where the people could imbibe its homely and practical lesson, would be as great an education to our people as the founding of a national university. It is not our intellects that need awaking; it is our souls.

Whenever the kind Fate who spins the thread of life brings you to "The Lovely Little Plain," pray for a rainy day. There will be fine ones in plenty when you will trudge over the mountain to the quaintly beautiful little village of Unterseen, with its old, old houses and its fine views of the peaks of the Mönch and the Eiger. You will climb to the ruins of Goldswyl, and look down at the gloomy depths of the Faulensee; or to Bönigen, concealed amid its orchards; or to the desolate castle of Unspunnen; or to the Heimwehfluh and the Rugen. And you will investigate the treasures of the small shops, with their ivory carvings and wood, their Alpine cowbells of silver and gold, their alpenstocks and photographs, and their many bewildering temptations for the purse. All this hay you will make while the sun shines—but none the less continue to pray for a rainy day.

For then all through the morning and late afternoon the warm, moist air will be more heavy than ever with odours of the woods and gardens, and below the dark precipices of the mountains the pale vapour of mist rises like incense before those altars of God, half hiding, half revealing their grandeur. You will walk between the showers, for the porous, sandy soil scarce holds the water while it is falling, and five minutes after one could promenade in ball slippers. The band in the Kursaal will play as usual, while you sip your coffee or your beer, and rest between two expeditions. All the world of fashion will be abroad, for rain frightens no one here any more than in Ireland. Then suddenly as you stroll along about three or four o'clock, there will fall a great glory from on high round about you; and lo! the Jungfrau, in all her splendour, shining between the dark gorge of the hills, and the mists, like aspirations, ascending into the blue heaven, and a dazzle of freshness and light everywhere. It is the most heavenly transformation. Your breath goes in a spasm of wonder and delight. Your eyes fill, and your heart also, in passionate regret that the dear world at home is not near to share and to heighten the ecstasy of feeling. And it will probably be that same evening, hours after the valley is in shadow, and the faint, last light is creeping higher and higher up the gloomy sides of the Breitlauenen, that the white brow of the Virgin will take on a faint rosy flush like the heart of a blush rose, and you will for the first time know the magic of the Alpen glow.

CHAPTER XX.

LUCERNE.

LUCERNE is almost too well-bred. Both the place and the people have an air of being always in full dress. The promenade along the quays is so elegant, the hotels behind it so fine—and so dear—the ladies and gentlemen who patronise them so very fashionable, that it strikes terror instead of delight into the heart of the modest, sentimental traveller. Before you are conscious of its beauty, you are overpowered by its deportment. There is nothing individual about it at first sight. It might be a French town, or an Italian, as well as a Swiss. There is no personal flavour to identify it. So the first day of your advent finds you ill at ease; half afraid you have made a mistake; wholly convinced that you will correct it by flying away next morning. The ocean of English, too, submerges you. In the best hotel, the Schweizerhoff, there are only British names on the register, British voices in the halls, British eyes and eye-glasses to gaze upon you, as your small self and smaller properties descend from the omnibus before the grand staircase. And that impassive British stare is so trying when it goes travelling abroad!

But the dinner is very good, and the dining-hall beautiful, looking out in the sunset on the lovely flower garden upon which the large windows open; and afterwards the orchestra plays among the palms and rhododendrons, while twilight fades over the lake, and the wonderful outline of Mount

Pilatus cuts like an etching into the luminous sky. Those who have seen the Bufa of Zacatecas, and who will imagine it increased ten-fold, twenty-fold, can have some idea of this towering, sombre ridge, as it looms over the city at nightfall. So you begin to grow, if not more content, at least less uneasy. You are satisfied to wait and see what the morrow will bring forth. And the morrow dawns like a revelation. The air is translucent; the wide esplanade by the lake side laughs in the royal wealth of sunshine. The limpid, dazzling water bathes the feet of the mountains; the blue haze of distance clothes their majesty in such tender loveliness that one's heart goes out to them in love and longing; the pretty bright steamers skim like darting flies to every point of the compass. The ladies come down to their morning coffee in light muslin or unobtrusive foulard; the gentlemen stamp in with hobnailed shoes and sturdy calves showing under knickerbockers; the pretty girl who is your *vis-à-vis* unbends in a kindly word of greeting. A hundred different plans for a hundred different forms of sensible adventure are in the air, and you can choose between them.

It is Ruskin, and not Murray or Baedeker, that the tourist should carry near his heart in going through Switzerland. It is he who is the Prophet of the Mountains; they are but the signboards. He has caught the spirit of their language; they, in their poor patois, but stumble over the words. The poorest copy of his delightful chapters is better than all the medley of maps and facts within the brave red covers of the others, even when they grade your admiration for you beforehand, as they do your purse, with one, two, or three stars. For what doth it profit a man if he gain the whole world of names and statistics, and lose the soul of the wonders they designate? What matter if he know from the rising of the sun to the going down thereof the height and depth of every peak and precipice, if he only learn to recognise them as so many feet of rock or snow, and is satisfied to remember them by dimensions instead of heart throbs.

Personally I have a grudge against Baedeker, he is so peremptory and omnipresent. There is no getting away from him if he once joins your company. Your route is laid out like the list of a washerwoman with every article counted and checked. So many days, so many places; so much money, so much good cheer. Here you are to turn to the right, there to the left. This spot you are to look upon at sunrise, and the other at sunset. For Heaven's sake, is there nothing to be left to chance or inspiration! Is there no loophole for that delicious feeling of satisfaction which warms your very soul when it seems that you yourself unaided and unguided have stumbled upon some rare and unknown spot? Suppose one begins his Swiss travels at the opposite end, or at one of the sides, instead of the route laid out for him. Is he to go backward or sideways like a crab in order to keep up with his guide, philosopher, and friend, Baedeker? A fig for all red covers! Let us be our own couriers.

There will not be the slightest danger of coming to grief. Go through Switzerland as you will, there is nothing but beauty before you. In the most out of the way and distant bypath, as well as in the highways of travel, there is satisfaction for the senses, uplifting for the spirit. Take that little valley of the Noisy Brook, into and out of which we sped yesterday on the way to more famous scenes. What a revelation of picturesque novelty it was. An entrance through one of those steep gloomy chasms, through which the river alone has been able to force a passage; then a sudden widening as if the rent walls were drawn backward, and in the space between the loveliest fields and meadows, in such bright light green that the world seems in gala dress. Scattered among them the homes of herdsmen and farmers. On one side, up to the very top of the dizzy height, the mountain pastures were set like emeralds in the dull framing of fir trees; tiny chalets of whitewashed stone and dark wood, with wide projecting roofs, dotted the steep slopes where it appeared impossible for human foot to tread. On the other, a perpendicular wall of rock, straight as El Capitan in the Yosemite, rose rampart-like at the edge of the rocky way, and down its black sides shot the silver arrows of numberless cataracts, all broken into white mist before they reached the undulating floor of the earth. The murmur and splash of these falling waters were everywhere; and the beautiful, filmy waves of spray, blown like smoke through the air, sweetened the glaring summer day to coolness. In the fields the grass was ripe, and every being capable of work in the hamlet was abroad cutting and tossing the fragrant harvest. Even the short, broad-bladed scythes, and queer three-pronged wooden forks, gave the fields an unusual aspect, and changed them from the well-beloved meadows of home, sweet and odorous in memory. With just such implements the forefathers of this people, a dozen generations back, must have tilled these happy slopes, while the same eternal heights looked down upon them. By the doors of wayside cottages old women and little children sit making bobbin lace, or embroidering those wonderful bits of fine needlework for which the country is famous. It must be the healthy activity of so much outdoor life which saves the people from blindness as a race, when one considers the infinite care and delicacy of sight necessary for the work, which occupies them through the long winter, of watchmaking, wood-carving, and lace; but so far we have seen few weak eyes, and no glasses. To be sure, the houses, large and small, are riddled with windows, and mountain air for six months in the year is a grand corrective for the seclusion of the other six; yet the fact remains astonishing.

Now it might not have spoiled our pleasure to know that

this enchanted valley was waiting us beyond a turn in the narrow road; that the cascade which broke in a sheaf of white foam from the eternal ice-fields of the glaciers was in some respects the most wonderful of all in Switzerland; that the rocky fortresses which barred the entrance lifted their battlements two thousand feet nearer heaven than the spot our own profane feet were treading, and that all this divine surprise of beauty and majesty had been named and catalogued long ago. But at least it would have moderated our transports, which are yet in that happy state of enthusiasm and astonishment which Johnson endeavours to snub by defining as "novelty acting upon ignorance." This is a much better frame of mind than indifference, the genesis of which might be stated as "novelty acting upon stupidity." Ignorance may be easily corrected, but stupidity is a congenital deformity.

But to return to our city. Day by day of the too short week you have left for it, new delights spring up about you. Bands of students on a vacation ramble, with flowers in their hats, come through the bright streets to the swinging chorus of a college song; a company of school-boys, armed with alpenstocks, answer with hurrahs from the deck of a passing boat. Some one of a thousand forms of sympathy with nature inebriates you and fascinates, until the plan of departure would be indefinitely postponed, if will could force necessity. Behind the width and grandeur of the boulevards come the dear, narrow, homely streets of the ancient city, with their wealth of history and romance. In one rises the old church of St. Leodegard, rich in stained glass, and sculptured stalls, and rarely carven walls, and one of the finest organs in the world. Whoever has heard one of the concerts given by the Kappelmeisters each evening during the season, has added a new memory to those that will live for ever. In another spot, that most wonderful national monument, the Lion of

Lucerne, lies in his lofty niche among the rocks over the pine-bordered lake. There are numberless places, full of interest as relics of old customs: the Kornmarkt; the Gothic fountain that has stood for 400 years in the Weinmarkt; the Stadthaus, with its venerable portraits of the magistrates who in time past ruled the fortunes of the city. There, too, is the fascinating Spreuerbrücke, which has come down from the fifteenth century, with its thirty-six pictures of the Dance of Death on the beams under its quaint roof. With all these to study, as well as the fortifications on the hill built in the year 1409, and the round tower below, which used to be part of the ancient ramparts, how sorry you will be when implacable time bids you say good-bye to Lucerne.

There are many delightful spots wherein one may find relief from the rushing maelstrom of summer travel between this and Interlaken. The little lake of Brienz is one. Aside from Giessbach, which between its cascade and mountain has acquired continental celebrity, there are tranquil, wholesome retreats, perched on the slope of charming foothills above the crystal clear green water, which have all the inspiration of mountain air, with the quiet which is its best nerve tonic. Such are Bönigen and Goldswyl, and the lovely shore of Iseltwald, and pretty Brienz itself. Such, too, is each little hamlet along that wonderful pass of Brünig-Meiringen, at the head of the long valley of the Aare: Lungern with its pretty chalets nestled in green plains at foot of the mountains; Brünig with its cascades and clusters of sharp peaks; Sarnen with its historic record, its Landenberg, and the beautiful walks amid its fir-bordered heights. Each one of these can be made a point of departure half-a-dozen times a day for all the prominent resorts which surround them within the limits of a ten or twelve hours' excursion, by the small lake steamers or ordinary trains. The prices charged for travel are wondrously small.

CHAPTER XXI.

THE RIGHI.

IF it were ever allowed to make earthly happiness a theme for prayerful petition, or to storm the throne of grace for other than spiritual consolation, the good Christian might certainly incorporate with his orisons the desire to make the ascent of the Righi if he has never yet been so fortunate, or to do it again if the experience has been granted him before. Can it be, after all, wholly an earthly happiness, a simple piece of material well-being, which sets one's heart and soul beating in such unison with all good and great thoughts, which lifts one for the time being out of the narrow and sordid pressure of life into communion with the eternal? Let me give you the data of facts, and you can decide the metaphysical question for yourselves.

The morning was as exquisite as midsummer could make it when we sailed across the pale green waters of the Vierwaldstätter, set between lovely shores, which rise gently to its framework of smooth and rounded hills as if they had been graded into undulating heights and hollows. Beyond rose the mountains; on one side the black and awful crest of Pilatus cutting into the blue sky like the jagged fin of some mighty monster; on the other, the lofty and beautiful outline of the Righi, abrupt as a precipice on the nearer edge, sloping in fine massive terraces upon the other. In the foreground the velvet richness of grass and artistic grouping of trees gave an effect of lawns and parks about the villas they surrounded;

behind, with here and there a glint of snow upon their summits, the chain of mighty peaks, softened by the azure haze of summer, melted into the horizon in all the exquisite gradations of purple and amethyst that only mountains can assume. The little villages on the way were as picturesque as if some trained and benign hand had placed each in the spot where it should be most precious to artistic sense; the broad, dark roofs gathered about the square, grey tower, with its tapering, conical spire, like a flock of ravens. The landing-place at Vitznau is one of the prettiest of these hamlets. Every house is in its own bower of red and white roses. There is deep shade of walnut and spreading beech-trees; the hay was fresh in the fields; the potato patches a mass of blossoms. Even the little Acre of God around the church tower had none of the grimness which usually surrounds the place of death; it was a garden of bloom and fragrance, with every grave hidden under a network of vines and flowers, where birds sang and bees hummed and little children played.

From this the railway—which, on the principle of that at Mount Washington, is provided with a cogged wheel in the centre—mounts very steeply. I do not remember so sudden an incline in any of our eastern or western mountain roads. Cut into the rock at one side, the other looks down upon the peaceful valley it is leaving, the emerald waters of the lake, and the opposite chain of the Alps piled confusedly against the horizon. There is nothing forbidding in the ascent. Nearly all the way up the small home fields and farms follow the line of the track, cultivated to the extreme edge of the precipices upon which they rest, luxuriantly fertile and peaceful. It is only the last quarter of the way which becomes less thickly covered with grass, and in which occasionally a bare or rocky spot is seen where some winter avalanche has torn away the soil. Beeches and walnuts growing slightly smaller, mingle with the hemlocks to within a few hundred feet of the summit, when all tree life stops rather suddenly. But to the end there is still a good sod, sown thickly with wild flowers; and there is none of the savage, biting cold which at a height of even six thousand feet makes our peaks at home such bitter experiences. As the line of road turns, different points come into view, but the direction is so largely the same that the summits which first dominate the landscape continue to be its most prominent features. At each of the six stations at which stops are made, very comfortable hotels and pensions, at exceedingly cheap rates, invite the tourist for whom the higher altitude and higher prices may be too great strain; and there is not one which has not the requisites for healthful rest and delightful outlook. With our ideas of mountain houses, these pretty spots, with flower gardens, terraces, glass-covered piazzas, and surrounding forests, seem wonderfully reasonable. Ten times each day the train ascends and descends, while the loveliest of wood paths, crossed here and there by rustic bridges, over tumbling cascades and brawling streams, invites one to exercise.

Every hundred feet of the road lifts one into new delight. The air, which was sultry below, becomes fresh and perfumed with the resinous spiciness of evergreens; a sudden rift in the rock wall at the side gives time for one fearful glance down a thousand-foot precipice; a short tunnel launches one upon a suspended bridge over a dark gorge, with a dashing torrent roaring below. Girls in the picturesque peasant costume of the Bernese Oberland, or the Unterwald, offer straw-braided baskets filled with fresh strawberries, or great black cherries bound in bunches, like grape clusters, or posies of Alpine roses and Edelweiss, or the wild Forget-me-not. The hand is stretched out for money as often in Switzerland as in any other portion of Continental Europe; but there is always something in it to give in return. There is the bouquet of flowers, or the leaf filled with fruit, or the web of hand-wrought lace, or the bit of carved wood. It is barter, not beggary, that meets you here. And why should not a thrifty people strive to glean from the rich harvest of strangers, gathered from every field of the distant unknown world, whatever they can honestly manage to give value for. It must be said in justice to the people that they are not importunate. A single negative will silence the boldest; a look is sufficient for most. If the amount of overcharge to which the summer tourist is obliged to submit in our country, and the fees it is customary to give hotel servants, were put in the balance and weighed against the few centimes demanded here and there—always with an equivalent offered—through Switzerland, we should be surprised to see how much more our republican simplicity demands of its pleasure-seekers by way of payment. A franc will go as far in donations here as a dollar across the water.

At the final station, a hotel which would do credit to any lowland city is perched upon a small plateau not a hundred feet from the summit of the Righi. Its rooms are large, well-furnished, and comfortable in every way; its salon and other public apartments beautifully fitted; its dining hall of fine dimensions, with a lofty ceiling, and a green and gold decoration which is highly effective. A broad flight of steps leads to it from the small station; there are outside balconies and verandahs, a blooming flower-garden is at either side of the hall door, and a more than excellent dinner of seven courses gives the finishing touch to the requirements of a good hotel. With your back turned to the outer world, you could not tell that you were not being served at any first-class house from Basle to Geneva. You could not be more carefully happed from any evil chance as regards rest or refreshment. Many a Paris restaurant famed for its table, serves colder soup and staler salmon than this inn of the Righi-

Kulm, 5904 feet above the level of the sea. With your back turned, this is what first strikes you; but now face about. Here is what you have come to see, instead of soft couches and plentiful tables. Regard it long and well, for probably the broad earth does not hold another more wondrous picture.

Look first before you. A tempestuous ocean of mountains, the crest of each storm-black wave dashed with snowy foam, with white flecks of scattered spray still clinging to their massive sides. You, upon the highest billow of all, half dizzy with the infinite height and depth which flying cloud and pale wraiths of rising vapour make to surge about you. Here and there, from some awful, nearer gorge, a mounting, smoke-like mist, as if from the hidden mouth of a crater, or a fathomless ravine which seems to plunge into eternal space among the sea of grey cloud-drift which fills it. A great calm of silence and peace. A sky of pale blue with shining clouds piled above the horizon, one of which dips now and again, blotting out in a haze of oblivion some portion of the visible world. Then again ridge beyond ridge, to the nearest edge of heaven, the wondrous sweep of this glorious sea, which seems to bridge the space between time and eternity. Walk to the other side of the little plateau and look in the opposite direction. Still the mountains; but this time with a vision of reposeful fields and quiet farm-houses between you. Low down in the green valley, the beautiful cross shaped Sea of the Four Cantons lies smiling in intense blue light from this distance; nearer, the emerald lake of Zug stretches to the very base of the great precipice upon which you stand; farther off the smaller waters of Egeri and of Alpnacht lie darkly shining in the shadow of the heights above them. The gloomy and frowning brow of Pilatus, black as if a remnant of its own dark tradition for ever clung about it, rises well in front; behind the swelling billows mount and toss until they break against the horizon. What contrast between the laughing, wide-stretching plain, and the desolation of these lonely solitudes which overhang them. Now a thick, grey mist blows down from some mighty peak, and part of the solid earth disappears in a vaporous whirlwind; again, in the twinkling of an eye, you are enveloped in a bright, soft haze, which engulfs all the world except the one rocky platform upon which you stand. Soon, first in this direction, then in that, a long cloud telescope opens like the slide of a magic lantern to show some glimpse of the happy valley, lying, still bathed in sunshine, below; soon, again, as swiftly as it came, the clinging veil disappears, blown into some other crevice, and you are standing on the sunny height, with one of the most beautiful visions in all God's beautiful creation spread before you.

If you are fortunate—and you probably will be—there will come to you, as you stand lost in this absorbing mood of contemplation, a strain of far away music falling at intervals, and at intervals swept away by the mountain breezes. It will draw nearer and nearer, its fitful sweetness merging into continuous harmony, until it sweeps in a fine wild melody around the brow of the mountain, and lo! a party of school children out with their teachers for a holiday frolic. They have clambered up the five miles of mountain-side like so many young goats; their alpenstocks are overtopped with gay bunches of mountain flowers; there are nosegays at their breasts, and trailing wreaths above their broad straw-hats; their cheeks are in a fine flame of enthusiasm and heat, and the clear pure air of the summit bandies their joyous nonsense about with a thin sweet iteration that belongs to the rarer atmosphere. They rush in a half frenzy of exultation from one point to another apparently as free from fatigue as if they had just stepped out of bed; and in clamorous, voluble French and

German, point out to each other the landmarks of the lower country spread like a vision at their feet. They will feast like kings at the hotel table by-and-by; sing one or two of their part-songs with the innate purity of intonation which seems to be born in this race; and run down the five miles between this and the landing again in the late afternoon, as fresh as the mountain air, and as jolly as grigs. Alack and well a day! Think of our young American palefaces after a ten-mile scramble! There would be nothing left of them but nerves and temper for the next fortnight.

The country upon which one thus looks from the top of the Righi has an interest greater than any loveliness alone could give it, from the fact that it is the cradle of Swiss independence. It was in these narrow valleys within their rocky heights, that the idea of freedom came 600 years ago, which has been held so tenaciously ever since. The Haut and Bas Unterwald preserve to this day probably the truest and least intricate form of republican government known in political history. On a green hillside overhanging the little capital of Sarnen, the people assemble on the first Sunday of April each year, and after a simple and dignified religious exercise, proceed to the direct election of the magistrates and rulers who are to guide their interests for the next twelve months. Every voter has the right to make his personal appeal for or against the candidate in question; and this right is used both with intelligence and moderation. The elder men have the honour of bearing the banner of the canton; the retiring officers, who are not admissible for re-election, make their annual statements, which are accepted or rejected; the hymn, "Come, Holy Spirit," is sung as an invocation of divine assistance, and under the blue, open sky, gathered in a semicircle about the White Cross of Switzerland, the election is concluded, and the people, with the new Landammann at their head, proceed to the parish church, where the priest asks the blessing of God upon those to whom temporal authority is for the time delegated. To be sure it is but a single canton of three or four thousand voters; yet compared even with a village caucus conducted in the ordinary manner, what sobriety, what earnestness, what dignity of action. It was at Sachseln near by, that the holy and reverend Nicolas de Flüe lived and died, as much revered by his countrymen for his loyalty to the idea of Swiss independence as for his piety. When in 1481 the young republic was in danger of destruction from internal dissension, it was his wise and loving hand which healed the breach and preserved the unity that has never been broken since. Why is it always among the highlands that such heroes and followers appear? What link between nature and the supernatural, allies mountains with liberty?

CHAPTER XXII.

GENEVA.

THE wanderer will find that the memory of Calvin is not more indelibly associated with Geneva than that of Voltaire. To leave the city without a visit to the famous château of the caustic wit and philosopher would be like omitting to look across the blue lake for the summit of Mont Blanc, rising in white grandeur beyond the dark precipices of the Great and Little Salève. It would be to forego any share in one of the crowning glories of the place. The little village of Fernex, which was in some measure of his creation, and the small property within its limits in which he spent so much time during the later years of his life, is really inside the French boundary, although its best known approach is from Switzerland. One reaches it by a delightful carriage drive of an hour and a half, by either of two different routes which are equally attractive, but for different reasons. The prettiest leaves the city through the Lane of Delight, a long, tree-shadowed alley running between high hedges of climbing rose and hawthorn bushes, which is an appropriate beginning for a pilgrimage of pleasure. A few miles of beautifully kept road across country—all these Swiss roads are marvels of construction and cleanliness—lead to a drive over the brow of a low hill rising directly above the water, giving a magnificent perspective of the long cloud-crowned range of the Jura on one side and the distant majesty of Mont Blanc on the other, with a foreground of deep sapphire water which floods the whole country side with dazzling luxuriance of colour.

On the finest portion of the hillside the beautiful domain given by Baroness Rothschild to the city as a retreat for convalescents lies in the midst of broad fields of grain; a group of greystone buildings, at once dignified and friendly, where pure air and sunshine can work their kindly mission. Adjoining is the Home provided for old people, with wide grounds and comfortable buildings, as little like the bare and stony institutions we are accustomed to connect with municipal charity as it is possible to conceive. Either property might be that of a private person, whose means and tastes were equally large. Later on a turn to the left introduces one to the main street of the picturesque village. Although so near the borders, it is decidedly French in its arrangement; even the wayside inn, with its swinging sign, announcing the "Hotel de Voltaire," is more auberge than chalet. There are several manufactories of pottery, mostly given to the production of household utensils, but including one of artistic pretensions. The front of the small house in which this industry is carried on, is ornamented with numerous plaques, brackets, jugs, and vases, with a decoration coarsely resembling the raised faience of Limoges; the flowers, birds, and figures well modelled, but the glaze clumsy, and the tints not pure. This workshop is popularly supposed to have owed its origin to the great writer, and its appearance indicates an age that might make such presumption possible. Somewhat farther on, a bronze bust of Voltaire surmounts the village fountain; and almost immediately afterward the short avenue leading to the château is reached.

At the end of the lane, behind a tall iron gateway, the small, white, two-story villa, still much the same in general outline as during its master's lifetime, rises in the midst of a narrow garden, planted with flowers and shrubs in the set fashion common to French horticulture. On one side an

artificial pond, with steps leading down, still shelters a
flock of ducks and a few swans, who sail majestically about
the fountain which ripples over a central pile of rocks, as
they used in the days when the greatest philosopher of the
time fed them with bread crumbs. On the other, the small
square chapel " Erected by Voltaire to God," as the inscription above its doors testifies—whether in mockery or refutation of the world's aspersion of atheism, who shall say ?—
shows its modest front under drooping foliage. A low flight
of steps to the right leads to the raised terrace at the back
of the house upon which the rooms especially consecrated to
his memory open. There are but two of these which have been
preserved in the order and condition in which he left them,
his parlour and sleeping-room. In the salon, dark in spite of
the light from a glass door and two small windows, are a couple
of sombre objects that would dim even a noonday sunshine.
One is the tomb, albeit in tiles and gilding, which reaches
from floor to ceiling, with an inscription reading, " My body
to France, my heart here." The other is an equally lugubrious and monumental stone, also in faience, also the full
height of the room, and bearing a bronze bust of the great
man atop. Four or five pictures on the wall, in oils, crayon,
or bas-relief, reproduce his features at different ages, but all
as like as peas in that smile half cynical, half arch, the high,
narrow forehead, and the expression of mingled insight and
dilettanteism. The furniture is embroidered in an intricate
design of fuchsias, the work of his nieces ; there are a few
bits of bric-a-brac and half-a-dozen paintings, gifts of famous
friends ; a faded carpet and some faded hangings, and that
is all. The smaller chamber, which opens from it, is of
greater interest. There is his small, low bed, the canopy
above still preserving the ragged remnant of former curtains
which have been hacked away piecemeal by relic hunters.
There is the picture of Queen Catherine, wrought in tapestry

stitch by her own hand, over the head board; another large life-size portrait of the same royal personage at the foot; a water colour of Frederick the Great on the wall at the side, and an oil painting of the hero in his uniform as general of the Russian army opposite. The philosopher's disdain for his great contemporary evidently did not extend to his counterfeit presentment. Over the mantel is an allegorical representation of the reception of Voltaire and Catherine into the company of the Immortals. About are some other small relics, with the reclining chair on which the frail nervous body so often lingered while the fiercely active brain worked upon the problems of life and thought. Outside, a small fountain throws a slender jet of spray into the sunshine; a quaint little summer house covered with Indian matting and adorned with faded paintings rises on one side, a deep tangle of wild woodland, of such thick growth that the tree trunks are black with moss for want of air and light, fills the other. Paths cut here and there show the direction in which his steps moved in abstract meditation; a great peacock, with argus-eyed tail spread proudly aloft, struts through them to-day. A few steps leading to a lower terrace, laid out now in a modern flower garden, with pretty stone balustrade, leads to the long, green alley formed of the closely interlaced boughs of trees, which was his especial and favourite promenade. So close have these Gothic arches of living green twined themselves together, that one might walk dryshod under them in the heaviest rain, although the gravelled floor is always moist beneath. The intense shadow is relieved by arched openings cut like windows on either side at regular intervals, through which the brilliant sunshine breaks in white patches. Walking slowly through this long, cool, green tunnel, flecked with alternate light and shade, one is reminded strongly of the intellect and temperament of him who created it, there are so many points of similarity between both. Not eschewing wholly either nature or God, he preferred to view both in a light which made them unreal. Alternately morbid and human, indulging in the most abstract philosophy and the brightest play of wit by turns, how like he is to this beautiful but strange construction, which is wholly artificial and yet wholly natural at the same time. From under the arched openings an exquisite view of Mont Blanc is obtained, rising like a luminous shadow to fill the pale distance beyond the valley and the lake. How often he must have paused in the midst of his deepest and bitterest reflections, called back by the glory of this vision to brighter thought and belief in the existence of the Supreme Power which had made earth so wonderful. Who knows how much the faith which led the brilliant cynic and scoffer still to retain allegiance to a Divine Being, was kept alive by the sublimity and graciousness of that wrapt presence set constantly before his eyes, and leading contemplation toward the upper atmosphere of the supernatural?

Returning to Geneva, one can choose the other route to and from Fernex, which skirts first another hill-slope with an especially beautiful view of the Jura, and then descends by the border of the lake, where for miles it passes among the villas of the great ones of earth, from the Rothschilds down to common millionaires. In this way one enters the city under the best conditions, coming immediately upon the fine quays or boulevards, which are bordered by the largest hotels and wealthiest private houses, and are everywhere surrounded by terraced flower gardens looking out on the wonderful blue waters of Leman. The Rhone, whose swift current passes through the lake as if through a walled passage, flows green and rapid under the bridges of the lower end past the Island of Rousseau and the open market-places. The streets are wide, sunny, well-paved;

bordered by dwellings more like the Parisian hotels, with their small balconies outside the long bright windows. The public spirit of the old citizens has helped to add elegance and charm to the town. The Musée Rath has a fine collection of modern pictures and bronzes. The Brunswick monument, although it commemorates a most unworthy character, is one of the ornaments of the city, with its beautiful garden and shaded paths. The Musée Foll contains a valuable collection of antiques; the Musée Epigraphique, within the Palace of Justice, has many interesting remains of the time of the Roman occupation of Geneva. The public gardens and promenades are many and various—one adorned with marble and bronze busts of celebrated Genevese; another above the Bastions, where occurred the historic Escalade, in which the citizen soldiers defeated the Savoyards in 1602. There is the English Garden, with its elegant little fountain and kiosk; the University, liberally open to female as well as male students, within fine grounds, which are free to the people; and numberless other spots terraced and tree-shaded, with those exquisite glimpses of the blue lake and deep background of misty mountains which make Geneva beautiful. The open flower and fruit markets, the Saturday fairs along the edges of the streets, the country carts drawn by ever-braying donkeys, the muzzled dogs, the constant sound of music from orchestras in the small café gardens or gathered on street corners, make the broad ways attractive to the stranger, while there are plenty of narrow paved alleys, entered under old archways which date from the earliest days of Genevese history, to repay the watchful search. Women will be glad to know that they can buy jewels at probably lower rates than anywhere else in Europe; men will not despise the fact that they can obtain suits as handsomely made as those of London, and decidedly cheaper. There is the theatre, which suggests the Grand Opera House of Paris on a small scale; the beautiful Casino, for those who would be gay; the quiet libraries and shaded walks for those who would be serious. Without exception the suburbs are delightful, rising above the city, with elegant villas and enchanting views of the lake and mountains.

Although Geneva shares so many features in common with Lucerne and Zurich in its foreground of dazzling water and background of soaring heights, it has a charm and glory solely its own in the presence of Mont Blanc shining beyond fifty miles of perspective. Perhaps no other view in Switzerland gives so wonderfully the relative values of its height and majestic outline as this. When in fine weather the eye roves through the clear atmosphere across the strangely blue sea, past the stony terraces of Salève, through the long sweeping lines of deep azure summits piled like battlements against a paler sky, to that dazzling culminating point which finally bars the field of vision, too far away for spot or stain to dim its serene purity, it is enough to set the least impressionable nature on fire with enthusiasm. The City is remarkable, too, for a certain appearance of belonging to its own people, despite the hosts of strangers who throng its rich and beautiful thoroughfares. No city in Switzerland gives the same impression of birth and breeding among its inhabitants; and this distinction of the householders is repeated in the houses themselves. The terraced gardens, bordered by the umbrella-like foliage of the plantain trees, adorned with statues and fountains, within which so many of finest Genevese homes withdraw themselves with a fine air of seclusion, are not to be found anywhere else: although here they are common enough to make one believe the largest portion of the people were born to the ways of wealth and leisure.

With much the largest proportion of their countrymen, even counting those who speak its language, the Genevese seem to dislike Germany quite as heartily as they like France. The feeling concerning the Teuton is well expressed in a witticism which is just now popular here. A Swiss peasant coming to town for the first time from his country hamlet stops before a picture of a monkey smoking. " Ach Gott! " he says, " what is that? It can't be an animal, for it has a pipe. It can't be a man, for there is its tail. It must be a German! " Some undefined doubt as to the intention or ambition of its grasping northern neighbour seems to dwell constantly in the imagination of at least the younger folk of the brave little freehold which is so close to it. But there is no fear. A people who have known how to preserve liberty for six hundred years will not easily lose the recipe. The topographical features of the country lend themselves so superbly to the idea of defence, that the old story of Thermopylæ might be repeated in every one of the dozen passes which guard these deep, peaceful valleys from intrusion. The country is a series of natural fortresses, and each can be made impregnable. For the sake of all who love the beauty and majesty of the world, it is to be hoped no possible political change will ever affect the republic. No other people could so understand the requirements of travellers, or make so easily feasible the delight of looking at this gracious and wonderful world. Such roads, such inns, such astonishingly low prices for the comfort and luxury offered, are known nowhere else.

CHAPTER XXIII.

CHAMOUNIX AND MONT BLANC.

No matter how much one has seen of Switzerland, he can never feel that he knows it intimately until he has taken some days' journey, at least, by diligence. The diligence belongs to the genius of the country as much as its glaciers and Alpine valleys. Imagine a great lumbering *char-a-banc*, with four high-backed seats each for four persons, so arranged as to face the horses, and a fifth for guards and drivers in front. The vehicle is so tall that one climbs into it on a ladder; the two seats in front are covered by a leather hood provided with glass windows, which can be closed in case of rain; the back benches are provided with awnings, and raised sufficiently high to allow the occupants to overlook the *coupé*. An immense van hung low between the wheels takes the luggage; and sixteen or eighteen passengers make the full complement. Imagine now six fine horses, three abreast, each with a high-peaked collar and a necklace of bells, and the team is complete. It easily travels forty or fifty miles between seven in the morning and six at night; horses being changed at stations of an hour's distance, and a stop of forty-five minutes made at some convenient station for lunch. To see this lofty thunderous chariot, with its horses at a swinging trot, rattling through the different country villages, with a jingling melody of bells, and a ringing volley of whip-cracking, as loud as a roll of musketry, with mothers and little children flying into protecting corners, and nods and smiles being interchanged between the brave coachman and his admiring friends, is to see a very fine sight indeed. But to be part and parcel of all this splendour is even a better experience. Now through long country roads fragrant with new-mown hay and briar roses; now through short close streets, where the homely smell of barnyards mingles with the sweetness of small house gardens; rattling under the hanging signs of the wayside inns, on a level with the second story windows; and convoyed everywhere by a rabble of small boys and girls with tempting baskets of raspberries and cherries—it gives the most delicious sense of rollicking motion one can well conceive. The wonderful roads are so clean and smooth that it is like driving through a park. The plains stretch away in luxuriant fields of grain and clover; every stony hillside is made into a smiling vineyard; the dark, fir-crowned mountains lead up to the eternal bastions of rock which mark the higher ranges; far in the blue distance, pale cloud peaks, with a glint of snow on their shadowy brows, make the horizon splendid. Between the beauty, the novelty, and the rushing sweep of pure cool air, life becomes an enthusiasm instead of a submission.

From whatever direction one chooses to approach it, the valley of Chamounix is reached through a constant succession of ascents and descents, gradually but almost imperceptibly mounting to the 4000 feet level upon which the base of Mont Blanc rests. Entering by way of St. Martin and Sallanches, the road winds between two parallel lines of mountain chains, skirts the edge of a deep ravine on a path half way up a steep hillside, and following the eccentric course of a rushing stream, enters the lovely village of Chamounix by a last swift turn over the pretty stone bridge of Saint Marie. There is a passing resemblance to the Yosemite in the appearance of the flat valley bounded by high ridges, with the river running through, especially if the mists hide the outline of the upper peaks from view. A most luxuriant vegetation covers every part of the floor of this sheltered nook in June. Wild flowers crowd the lower slopes; roses and honeysuckle twine in bowers of bloom around the small houses; the ridges of peas in the kitchen gardens are full seven feet high, and crowded with blossoms. Such a diversified and beautiful flora is scarcely to be seen on the plains of Lower California. Brilliant patches of forget-me-nots, Alpine roses, pansies, marguerites, bluets, buttercups, wild foxglove, blue gentian, violets, harebells, and primroses, decorate this small wilderness of loveliness. On the nearer Alps, herds of cows and goats, each with the faintly tinkling Alpine cow-bell about its neck, move slowly among the steep little pastures, which everywhere creep up amid the fir forests. The river looks more like a torrent of crushed snow than of water, as if the silent frozen streams of the glaciers above had been suddenly precipitated into movement. The houses are all picturesque, with wide spreading eaves, and roofs of brown shingle held down by great stones. On either side, a succession of sharp-pointed ridges run in parallel lines at right angles from the road toward the great ranges which rise behind. The whole aspect of nature is more gentle and soft than bold or awful.

We entered in a driving rainstorm, which hid all save this homely, quiet landscape from our eyes. The clouds shut out everything beyond the immediate low line of hills; children were running through the tall wet grass to call the cattle home; women sat knitting in the porches sheltered by the overhanging roofs. It was like a hundred other peaceful happy nooks we had passed in the day's ride—full of the look of content which these guarded nests seem to hold within the seclusion of the walls which seem to gather them away from the turmoil of the outer world. Half-an-hour afterward a darting ray of sunshine broke through the window of the room where we rested, and lo! the world was transfigured! The valley, which had seemed to be the only visible object, was gone, reduced to the merest foothold of green, from which sprang into the highest heaven one radiant presence, glowing with dazzling splendour, of which all other mountain soaring had been but the pale shadow. To attempt to describe the unearthly majesty of Mont Blanc in words to one who has never seen it, is like trying to convey to a child's mind some conception of the Deity by repeating over the names which have been given to His attributes. Speech is but a deaf and dumb alphabet with which to attempt the expression of emotions which spring from such sublimity. There is something at once so awful and beautiful, so soothing and overpowering in the presence of this royalty of nature, that one can but lift up the eyes and mutely adore as in the presence of the Eternal One. Once the magic of that vision has touched like chrism the awakened eyes, earth can never be quite the same again to the human soul which has received it. There shall never come a joy so complete but that this memory shall not remain a grace to its setting; there can never fall a sorrow so bitter that this remembrance cannot somewhat lessen its pain. Only to have once been allowed to look upon it, is a gladness to life for ever after.

How many times that first night we looked out, to be sure that the wonderful glory had not vanished, and slept again, content to have seen it under the stars as clearly as in the sun of noonday! How we watched it under the rosy flush of morning, while the white curtains of mist had not yet been withdrawn from the sleeping peaks below; what a short two days of silent homage we paid its inspiration as it put on with each hour some new enchantment, as a monarch clothes himself in the differing splendours of his robes of state? Which was fairest? Dawn, or sunset, or midday glow, or faint radiance of the young moon sailing down the western sky? Who can tell, or who would care to decide, once his eyes "have seen the glory of the coming of the Lord."

After the first glimpse of Mont Blanc, all else fades into insignificance. The long spurs of forest-crowned slopes making ladders from its white height to the valley; the shining rivers of glaciers falling in frozen billows of green and white light between them; the pastoral loveliness of the little plain, with its quiet farm-houses and flower-sprinkled pastures—what are they but the framing of that priceless gem above. They are the setting of the picture, and Nature never commits the solecism of making her shrines too ornate for the divinity to whom they are dedicated. But everything is harmonious, and blends with the principal impression. Even the sound of the tinkling sweet-voiced bells from the lowing herds wandering slowly homeward in the twilight, remains always part of one's pleasure in the place, and is never heard again without recalling it. And the little goat-herds, clambering down after their flocks with shrill clear cries, and yodels that fade away among the crags; and the small shepherdesses, with fair hair tightly braided, knitting their long stockings as they follow the flocks through the grass; and up and down the village street, the guides with cock's feathers in tall Tyrolese hats.

For ten or twelve miles after leaving the valley one still looks backward at the mountain. First from one angle, then from another; now a glimpse only, again a few moments of full view, it moves to left and to right, before and behind one, as the loveliest road in the world twists and turns through gorges and hillsides. The awful mouth of the Tête Noire swallows one awhile, then the road zigzags upon itself four different times, until it comes out a thousand feet above the valley, with the cataracts and whirlpools of the boiling stream below as motionless as the dusty white road beside it. But in the steepest, the wildest, the most remote spot, wherever there is an inch of soil, there is also the inch of cultivation; signs of human presence and loving labour soften the sternest outlook. At intervals the exquisite valleys enclose thrifty, clean villages, and wide fertile fields; at intervals, again, a rare bit of desolation glows like a mosaic of crimson and amber from the wild rhododendron growing among the yellow rocks. A southern slope is covered with the elegant foliage of the chestnuts, those aristocrats of trees; a forest of larches drapes the path like curtains of lace.

Down below, far away, one sees the village where the night is to be passed—one long street bordered with farm-houses set in the midst of the green plain, with a single snowy cascade falling like a long white plume over the dark brow of the mountains that hem it in. The wise man will pass through Martigny, even if the grey round tower on the height charm never so wisely, and go on to where fair Vernayaz rests at the entrance to the Gorge of Trient. There is nothing among the Colorado cañons more beautiful for its size than this 1800 feet cleft in the rocky walls that rise from 600 to 1000 feet in sheer perpendicular lines from the roaring torrent that tears its way through like an angry raging creature, breaking from bondage to light and freedom beyond. The cliffs approach to within six feet of each other in the narrowest place, and separate to perhaps eighteen in the widest. One wall is the beginning of the range of Mont Blanc; the other that of the Dent du Midi. It is the melted ice of the glacier which bursts between these at the farther end, in one superb bound of white wrath so fierce and strong that the stream in which it merges is forty feet deep as it hurls itself onward. A narrow wooden gallery is hung from the side of the wall along its whole extent, dimly lighted by the patch of blue sky that shines far above. Pale sprays of flowers bleached by the shadows in which they have grown, and clumps of maidenhair fern, hide in the crevices—the only break in the aspect of defiant sternness which marks the scene. It is hard to understand why so few people, comparatively, have seen a bit which is really one of the wildest expressions of savage nature in this portion of Switzerland, and which makes up in intensity what it lacks in extent. Outside, over the pretty plain of Vernayaz, one black mountain slope is perforated from top to bottom with holes like those of cliff swallows, where the slate quarries open from which a large part of the country is supplied. Happily it is the only development of resources we saw on the entire journey. One trembles to think what might happen if this world of wonderment and loveliness should suddenly prove to be a mass of mineral wealth. Would the Swiss soul, which is equal in exaltation of prudence to that of the canny Scot, prove capable of resisting the temptation; or would the soaring glory of the Matterhorn, and the majesty of the White Mountain, vanish in piles of rubbish and the dirty refuse of mining shafts? It is doubtful whether the diamond-fields of South Africa have been any greater source of wealth to those who discovered them, than the beauty of Switzerland to its peasantry. But it is a wise dispensation of Providence for the peace of mind of the æsthetic world, that the chance of amassing sudden and colossal fortunes in this way has not been offered the inhabitants. They might prove unable to resist the temptation.

We brought with us, by way of reminiscence, one of the small cow-bells which mark one of the pleasantest memories of Chamounix. I shall never hear it again without seeing, like some fair, far off vision, the lowing herds winding slowly through the deep pastures of the happy valley; the quaint little maids, flaxen-haired and demure, walking gravely behind, as they deftly ply their shining knitting-needles; the sweet peas climbing to the rude gables of the peaceful small houses; the rushing of the green torrent through the gloaming; and the awful mysterious beauty of that wonderful mountain lifted high above in the upper air, with the evening alpen glow crowning its white brow, as if the luminous shadow of the throne of God had for a moment rested upon it.

LONDON.

CHAPTER XXIV.

LONDON: AMONG THE LIGHTS AND SHADOWS.

HE who has eaten of the fruit of the tree of knowledge by becoming used to the routine of travel first in France and Switzerland, will feel that he has been driven out of paradise for many a long day after he has been forced to enter upon other scenes. The wonderful caretaking shown in road and street, the perfection of hotels, the comfort of the Pension, the unvarying courtesy of tradespeople and domestics, the facilities for journeying in every direction, and the exceeding cheapness, make a climax of perfections not easily forgotten. When the exquisite beauty and novelty of scene are added, and the sense of romance and pleasure which foreign costumes and a foreign tongue add to the ordinary experience of life, there is a zest given to enjoyment which is scarcely possible under other circumstances. No matter how delightful an English-speaking country may be, or with what homely felicity of remembered pleasures she woos memory, some evanescent perfume of imagination has escaped on the passage from Italian skies and Provence roses, that never comes again until they shine once more for us. That is to say, for certain temperaments. For others, like poor Blanche of Devon, there is neither rest nor thanksgiving, except upon the native soil and amid the soothing influence of the home atmosphere. But I think for most people the "eternal commonplace" of life, the wear and tear which belong to the narrow and uniform round of duties that go to make up everyday existence, vanishes more completely under the stranger surroundings.

Whether one tries hotels or lodgings, a little cloud seems to have settled over the world on this side of the Channel, as compared with that on the other. One misses the swift attendance, the bright smile, the cleanliness which seemed next to godliness, the flutter of the white lace curtains, the ever-present grace of flowers—one misses them as one would dear faces of familiar friends. It is a wearisome work to come back to the dirty corners and grimy heaviness of stuffed chairs and gloomy draperies; to the indifferent, stolid look which accompanies the indifferent service; to the bleeding, heavy rounds of beef, and fat legs of mutton. Something of the old care and moil returns; something of glamour and fascination departs. The shadow of the end of the holiday is approaching.

To classify London under any general heading of impressions is not only hard—it is impossible. Its size, by which one has expected to be overwhelmed, does not after all press so heavily upon the sense after Vienna and Paris. Two millions added to two millions scarcely impress one as being much greater. Nor is the roar, except when out in the midst of it, so very aggressive. But the enormous discrepancies, the impression of infinite luxury and infinite poverty, the evidences of wealth and of squalor which follow so closely on each other's footsteps, daze one. A tremor of awe seizes the soul and presses the imagination, as if one stood on the verge of fearful unknown possibilities. Here is a Museum rich with the rarest treasures of thought and knowledge, endowed with such infinity of resource and such lavish prodigality that it becomes one of the wonders and delights of the earth; there from its very gates stretches a street as encumbered with dirt, and grime, and strange woeful specimens of human wretchedness, in the labyrinth of foul lanes and vicious courts which lead into it, as would challenge Hogarth's pencil to caricature. There can be no extravagance of expression in describing London wretchedness, as there can be none in designating its splendour. One might walk for days among palaces wreathed in flowers, shining in plate glass and pillared portico, overlooking broad parks set with noble trees among which stately herds of deer wander; and almost anywhere upon the way, a turn to the right hand or to the left will bring one face to face with the same terrible unsolved problem of suffering. Then, again, from the midst of the most sudden and depressing neighbourhoods, with every evidence of want and crime, and that expression of sullen, dogged resentment which makes London poverty unlike any other on the face of the globe, a dozen steps under some obscure archway, an instant's swerving from the loud, filthy, brutal street, will lead you into blessed spots full of quiet and sunshine, brightened by memories of deathless names, or by the more precious evidences of living zeal and devotion. The richest pages of history offer their illustrations in the most dreadful neighbourhoods; the proudest arrogance of wealth jostles rags and tatters. It is this impression more than any other that the first weeks, and above all, the first days, leave uppermost.

But after this first inevitable confusion, this chaos of blended emotions, a certain balance begins to establish itself. With the help of the thousand and one smaller guide-books, devised like milestones to help the stranger toward the landmarks of his special interest, the tangled ways begin to clear. For the historian the wonderful background of centuries unrolls itself like the figures on the walls of a tapestried chamber, dim but tangible, to add the delightful test of actuality to the vagueness of research. From the old waterways of the Thames to the gloomy walls of the Tower, from court and palace and dim vaulted church aisles, the personages of his vision troop in serried ranks. Westminster Abbey gathers within its beautiful walls the glorified shadows of three hundred years; London Bridge and St. Paul's, the Temple and Whitehall, the Strand and Smithfield are before him yet, to repay every foot of his progress with priceless associations. For the literary man it is even more rich and complex. All that is dearest and finest to the English-speaking world, whether it be of wit or philosophy, poetry or art, has here its stronghold. To the burrower among books it is like coming home to some inheritance dear to heart and intellect just to pass over the sidewalks and read the names upon the street signs. A strange sense of pre-existence takes hold of one, as if in some earliest long-lapsed state all these things had been parts of previous being. It is not half as strange to us as New York or San Francisco. At every step one comes upon the footprints of some beloved ancestor, and the air is full of echoes of voices familiar and sweet to the ears. Not to the material sense of hearing in the present. That is tortured beyond expression. Insular English is not so wholly absurd as that which goes abroad for summer airing, but faith! 'tis bad enough. With many a delicious and sweet-voiced exception, for which heaven be devoutly praised, the Queen's English is most grievously battered and browbeaten by her most loyal subjects. There is little reason for any rule of pronunciation in Anglo-Saxon; but even that little is thrown to the winds by an eccentricity of speech which passeth all understanding. The vowel which is broadened out of shape in one sentence is minced into something frailer than air in another; the poor consonants are huddled together and submitted to hydraulic pressure this instant, and drawn out in extenuated single file the next; the voice tilts down in the middle of a sentence and up at the end—it is a miracle of unbridled absurdity. And this is leaving out the accidents of dialect and patois which should be supposed to belong exclusively to the common people. A Judge upon the Bench will talk of his "consti-*chew*-ency," and a learned counsel quote the "Coke Hurled" without fear of suit for libel from the *Cork Herald* he has so maligned; and people whose attainments, both socially and intellectually, would be a pride and honour to any society, mouth their sentences in a way which is delicious exercise for the imagination, but trying to common sense. Since this latter is rather a rare factor in observation, however, it is less to be pitied.

To the mind trained by reading and reflection it is impossible to move in London without intense gratification. It is like a triumphal progress through royal scenes with more than royal companions. A thousand times one is led to feel—

> "Not by appointment do we meet delight and joy—
> They heed not our expectancy;
> But round some corner in the street of life
> They clasp us, with a smile."

Amid the strangest belongings, these happy ghosts wait to greet us, until the power of human interest flags under the strain. To-day it is with kings and queens we walk; to-morrow with saints and martyrs; this moment we are with Johnson and Goldsmith in the Mitre Tavern and Wine Office Court, the next with Shakespeare in the Hall of the Temple, or Carlyle and Sir Thomas More by the river bank at Chelsea. Here, there, everywhere, the haunts he loves are about one; the treasures he delights in are open to him. He can revel in old bookstalls and print shops; he can feast his eyes on relics and manuscripts; he can make tangible his aspirations of years. And all the glory, the grandeur, the delight is familiar and dear, as belonging to the forbears of his own race and the pages of his own family history.

It is this which gives to it the last and crowning element of personal interest.

But to one who adds to this the kindly human feeling which binds man to his fellows, it is not so unmixed a pleasure. The pressure of human misery is too close, too awful. The more imaginative temperament and the stronger religious faith which cause poverty to be worn with so easy a grace, and lead its followers to accept so happily whatever is offered in its alleviation in other countries, is wanting here. There is an aspect of sullen antagonism, a hapless mixture of indifference and resentment in the faces about Seven Dials and Billingsgate, which is wholly unlike anything one meets elsewhere in Europe. There is also an abjectness of dirt in the sordid, filthy rags of the very poor; in the bleared faces and grimy hands; in the filthy lanes and passages among which they dwell, which is entirely new to the observation. The houses look far more comfortable outwardly than many of the quarters of Dublin, New York, and Paris; there are countless forms of attempted relief in green openings into parks and gardens, in every form of charity known to refined human sympathy, in missions and schools and friendly societies; but nothing lightens the dull, awful weight of the impression which the poor of London leave upon the heart. It is a moral oppression which colours all beauty, all splendour, as a lowering storm dims with sinister shadow the brightest summer landscape. The cloud will pass, leaving refreshment of purer air behind it; but, alas! what thunderbolt of eternal justice, what lightning flash of purifying grace, will ever clear this incubus, and what desolation will it leave in its track! I saw more the aspect of misery, the hideousness of sordid wretchedness, the brutality of passion, the partial forgetfulness of intoxication, in three days of London than I had in three months before; and the weeks after only deadened without obliterating the impression. In the play of the poor, pitiful little children, in the treatment of infants by fathers and mothers, there was a harshness and coarseness that never had been forced upon attention in other lands. And this at a time when enjoyment of its rich, varied, tremendous attractions for the higher nature was so overpowering that it should have usurped every other consideration. I think it would take a long time so to adjust the claims of sympathy and intellect, of soul and sense, as to make an observer's life in London come under normal conditions. To go, for instance, from the distinctly noble and Christlike work of Toynbee Hall, with the opening for spiritual and material light which has been created about it, into the lanes and halls of the Whitechapel district, which immediately surround it, foul with every moral and physical degradation from sewer smells to murder, is to be lifted too high and sunk too low on the billows of emotion to be able to keep a healthy poise of thought or feeling. Yet in some form or other it is to this strain one is every day subjected. Even the manner in which, when a fee or an alms was in question, it had the appearance of a demand rather than a request, and the scowl or the curse if it were not forthcoming was in harsh contrast to the half-jesting, half-earnest clamour of the Irish beggar, or the polite bit of wheedling, under the guise of *pour loire*, to which one is subjected in France and Switzerland. The sentiment in the heart of all these poor wretches may be the same, and the sullen resentment at fortune in the Englishman's face may hide below the surface in his Celtic or Gallic neighbour, but it gives a bitterness to the stranger's estimate of the people which is hard to efface; and so long as poverty must remain in the world, one cannot help wishing with all one's heart that the harsh line which separates it from riches should not be made more darkly prominent than it really is. Many different things in the political economy of kingdoms and empires puzzle the republican simplicity that is brought face to face with them for the first time; but the expression of antagonism to existing conditions, whether of men or things, that is written upon the face of the poor of London is hard to comprehend. There is only one thing harder, and that is the look of sullen and hopeless misery which sometimes takes its place, and blots out all appearance of human emotion from the unfortunate creatures who seem to retire behind it as behind a mask or a fortress.

CHAPTER XXV.

LONDON: IN THE FOOTSTEPS OF THE GREAT.

NOTHING in London strikes the American quite so strangely as the absence of strangeness. One is amazed each instant at the familiar aspect of names and places, and the persistency with which they meet one. Here the "Howell and James" young men of "Patience" look through their plate-glass windows; there Day and Martin shine with black brilliancy; now a scent of the toilet-table lingers about the birthplace of Pears' soap; then a delicious, all-pervading atmosphere of raspberry jam and mixed pickles emphasises the neighbourhood of Crosse and Blackwell. Perfumery and flannels, ale and Albert biscuit, mackintoshes and umbrellas —this is the book of Genesis for all. It is like reaching the cradle of the race of inanimate things.

As for the feast of reason and flow of soul, it is everywhere. Here is the church in which Hazlitt was married; there the house where Lamb lived. Up this dark alley Goldsmith and Johnson walked arm-in-arm from Fleet Street, with snuffy, listening Boswell close behind. Pass out of Bolt Court into Gough Square, and you can climb up the stairs, holding by the very banisters which often supported the gouty hand of the short-winded, short-tempered, big-hearted old philosopher. There is the room in which the great dictionary was compiled; and the quaint, dingy fireplace, by which the lonely man used to sit after the death of his wife, with his tea brewing on the hob, and the small circle of stout friends around him. Down that little paved lane is the famous Inn of the Cheshire Cheese wherein he was used to smoke his pipe and drain his tankard of bitter ale with Reynolds and Burke. At the upper end of the long table the mark of his greasy peruke is still to be seen upon the dark wainscoting, and the arm of the old bench is worn with pressure of the heavy leaning elbow as he alternately brooded and discoursed. The floor is fragrant yet with sawdust as it used to be in his day; light struggles through the same small paned windows; the same famous beefsteak and kidney-pie graces the five o'clock dinner; the two guinea punch-bowl holds the historic brew which served as ambrosia for these gods of old. One can fancy it might be the same waiter, with his mutton-chop whiskers, who whispers in a husky voice legend after legend of those halcyon days for your delectation, who brings you the best grill in London just popped from the gridiron to your plate, with a nibble of cheese and a pewter noggin of 'alf an' 'alf, and who drops his h's with an unforgetting imperturbability that commands your respectful admiration. It does one's very soul good to have reached a station on the journey of life where the inconveniences and eccentricities of the olden times have held their own against the pressure of modern improvements; where on high festival nights, tallow-candles are still used instead of gas; and the wooden benches are as hard and uncouth as they were a hundred years ago. There is need of but little imagination to fill the musty, awkward little bar, and the low room beyond, with shades of jolly good fellows from Herrick and Rare Ben down to Wilson and Southey, De Quincey and Coleridge. The spot is made for them.

Then there is the Temple—not the gorgeous new Law Courts that fill the opposite side of the Strand, where Temple Bar used to stretch its ancient arch above the moil of modern traffic; but that beautiful inner labyrinth of courts, alleys, and quadrangles which stretches around and beyond the wonderful Church of the Knights. The Temple, with its fair bright gardens reaching down to the river embankment; the well-beloved Goldsmith's grave resting under the ivied shadow of the chapel walls; the great dining hall in which Shakespeare read his Twelfth Night to Elizabeth, and the Virgin Queen danced a measure with Sidney and Raleigh! It is such spots as these which make London precious to memory, full of such wealth of association, such blending of history and romance, as make one lead a dual life while lingering among them. O the quiet and deep peace of those Temple Gardens, when turning in from the roar of the Strand, a dozen steps lead one into the restfulness of seclusion and green trees, and nodding flowers and ripple of bird song! It is impossible to conceive greater contrast. There the unlovely rush and hurry of material existence, the fret and anxiety of toil, the bewildering roar and bustle of mighty interests, which surge and sweep as if individual affairs were but straws to be tossed away on the inexorable current. And here the calm of contemplation, the open blue eye of the sky, the tender face of nature pressed so close to ours that we can read her soul. It is like a plunge from the garish chaos of Time to the clear penumbra of Eternity, to wander through the aisles of the dim old church, or among the lofty shadows of the hall, with Vandyke's King Charles riding in royal state out of the gloom, or beside those unknown graves whose occupants have so long vanished from human sight, that they do not even arouse human sorrow.

One can float down the river from foot of these same gardens, taking boat, as those men of old might have taken theirs to other scenes of loving remembrance; gliding past the beautiful towers and gracious outlines of the Abbey and the Parliament Houses to Chelsea. There, beyond the little square which now holds his bronze effigy, is the street which bears Carlyle's house, with his gloomy mask set as a trademark into the outer wall. How he would have despised such a claim upon the attention of passers-by. It is not nearly so sad a spot as the imagination of its owners made it. The low fence which bounds the opposite side of the street allows a more than usual amount of sunshine to fall upon the narrow, three-storied building, gay now with ledges of flowers in every window, and showing a cool glint of greenery through the passage way from the open hall door to the back garden. It looked like a spot that could have been made not only a happy but a bright home for natures not so overborne by the shadows of genius. A little less dyspepsia or a little more content would have made a different estimate of their surroundings in the minds of Jenny Welsh Carlyle and that great unhappy man who was her husband. It needs but a look at the powerful, keen-tortured face of the statue in the square above, with the loose coat twisted like an invalid's robe around the frail, worn figure, and the unconscious expression of dissent and antagonism which breathes from every line of the pose, to understand that it would have been difficult for such a spirit to be in touch with its surroundings even if they had been those of palaces.

Only a little way around the corner are the former abodes of others whom our reverence delights to honour. Dante Gabriel Rosetti once lived there, and George Eliot; while farther down the same Cheyne Walk was the sweetest and kindliest nature England ever gave to the world, Sir Thomas More. What a different earth this would be if nature more often moulded her heroes on the lines of this great, generous, loving figure, whose serene, smiling philosophy, and noble faith, no perversity of chance or misfortune could tarnish! And what blissful barter for the snarling Scottish giant, could he have exchanged a portion of his golden intellect—precious indeed, but harsh and cruel—for the warm radiant heart, pulsing with love for man and faith in God, which beat within the bosom of his neighbour!

But in this sort of reminiscence London is so rich that to follow it would fill the days for months without turning to right or left for intercourse with the present. The pavement of the city streets as well as the crypts of the churches are rich with a mosaic of threads which run through the entire warp and woof of history. In the darkest and dullest corners of the city one stumbles upon traces of characters and events so glorious that they brighten the dullest clouds of material environment. There is scarce a figure dear to the heart of the student, the patriot, the philanthropist, or the reformer, which does not cast its luminous shadow on these grimy walls and make the dull skies radiant. It is in this way, that with little or none of the material charm which captures sense and imagination in the continental cities, it fascinates by mere force of association. Its dirt repels, its poverty shocks; its air of brutal wealth as well as of brutal misery makes the heart sick; the smoke-dark heaven and soot-grimed houses cloud the sensitive appreciation which have been fed upon beauty and brightness. But in spite of all, it takes hold of something deeper and stronger that belongs to the soul of the Anglo-Saxon race. The Tower, Westminster, St. Paul's, the Museum, Kensington, Sydenham, the parks, the monuments, the galleries, the palaces, are such a rare and strong world of their own. Most of it has been so familiar to us across the water by picture and description from childhood that it is like looking upon the face of an old friend to enter upon it for the first time.

But after all, there is more gratification as well as greater novelty about the hidden by-paths which are yet fragrant with the memories of nearer and dearer brethren—bright souls whose glory is more intimately our own than even kings or heroes. In these the city is richer than words can tell. In the older portions, there is no spot of earth which is not hallowed by their footsteps, and the interest in following them is absorbing. There are other impressions, too, which should not be missed. The service at the Foundling Hospital is one, where the children's voices are nearer the sweetness of the angelic chorus than will ever fall on human ears this side of heaven; and where the children's faces are more full of the innocent careless grace of childhood than I ever remember to have seen among those trained by that cold stepmother, Charity. There are the Blue Coat Boys of Christ's Hospital; and the Charterhouse, which was the Alma Mater of so many brilliant sons; and the People's Palace, which sprang like an enchantment from the tip of a magician's pen. Then there is the Universities Settlement of East London, which is sketched in the story of Robert Elsmere. This admirable institution of Toynbee Hall is in itself alone enough to counteract and hallow a large share of the grievous impressions which the ordinary aspect of London makes upon the stranger. The affiliation of culture with ignorance, and of trained moral sense with the obtuseness of unawakened conscience, is capable of producing great results; and the principle of seizing hold of and occupying the mind before the attention has been caught by debasing pleasures and unworthy aims is fundamental. Toynbee Hall, built in the midst of the most degraded and wicked district of Whitechapel, is not for purposes of reclaiming, but of prevention. The young university men who take up their abode and go on with their regular work within its walls mix freely with the people, become their friends and counsellors, introduce them to healthy recreations, wholesome reading, cleanliness of body, purity of mind, clearness of conscience. It is not by any means an intellectual training simply which they suggest and offer, but a wider and fuller awakening of all the traits which go to make up nobler manhood. Any one who visits the small pretty enclosure, like a minature Oxford quadrangle in which a love of beauty is as carefully cultivated as a love of higher things, and who sees the interested awakened faces of those who have been helped to a better understanding of the claims of existence, can scarce fail to be touched by the evidences of earnestness and sincerity all about him. It is one of the fairest sights in London, and its memory will live when the sinister effect of its pomp and degradation, riches and misery, shall have faded for ever.

THE END.

BRIGHT AND BREEZY BOOKS OF TRAVEL
- - - - BY SIX BRIGHT WOMEN - - - -

MEXICO — PICTURESQUE, POLITICAL, PROGRESSIVE
By MARY E. BLAKE and MARGARET F. SULLIVAN. Cloth, $1.25.
"This is a very charming volume. The writers went through the country with their eyes wide open, and they have the faculty of interesting others in what was of interest to them."

A WINTER IN CENTRAL AMERICA AND MEXICO
By HELEN J SANBORN. Cloth, $1.50.
"A bright, attractive narrative by a wide-awake Boston girl."

A SUMMER IN THE AZORES, with a Glimpse of Madeira
By Miss C. ALICE BAKER. Little Classic style. Cloth, gilt edges, $1.25.
"Miss Baker gives us a breezy, entertaining description of these picturesque islands. She is an observing traveller, and makes a graphic picture of the quaint people and customs." — *Chicago Advance.*

LIFE AT PUGET SOUND
With sketches of travel in Washington Territory, British Columbia, Oregon, and California. By CAROLINE C. LEIGHTON. 16mo, cloth, $1.50.
"Your chapters on Puget Sound have charmed me. Full of life, deeply interesting, and with just that class of facts, and suggestions of truth, that cannot fail to help the Indian and the Chinese." — WENDELL PHILLIPS.

EUROPEAN BREEZES
By MARGERY DEANE. Cloth, gilt top, $1.50. Being chapters of travel through Germany, Austria, Hungary, and Switzerland, covering places not usually visited by Americans in making "the Grand Tour of the Continent," by the accomplished writer of "Newport Breezes."
"A very bright, fresh and amusing account, which tells us about a host of things we never heard of before, and is worth two ordinary books of European travel." — *Woman's Journal.*

BEATEN PATHS; or, A Woman's Vacation in Europe
By ELLA W. THOMPSON. 16mo, cloth. $1.50.
A lively and chatty book of travel, with pen-pictures humorous and graphic, that are decidedly out of the "beaten paths" of description.

AN AMERICAN GIRL ABROAD
By Miss ADELINE TRAFTON, author of "His Inheritance," "Katherine Earle," etc. 16mo. Illustrated. $1.50.
"A sparkling account of a European trip by a wide-awake, intelligent, and irrepressible American girl. Pictured with a freshness and vivacity that is delightful." — *Utica Observer*

CURTIS GUILD'S TRAVELS

BRITONS AND MUSCOVITES; or, Traits of Two Empires
Cloth, $2.00.

OVER THE OCEAN; or, Sights and Scenes in Foreign Lands
By CURTIS GUILD, editor of "The Boston Commercial Bulletin." Crown 8vo. Cloth, $2.50.
"The utmost that any European tourist can hope to do is to tell the old story in a somewhat fresh way, and Mr. Guild has succeeded in every part of his book in doing this." — *Philadelphia Bulletin.*

ABROAD AGAIN; or, Fresh Forays in Foreign Fields
Uniform with "Over the Ocean." By the same author Crown 8vo. Cloth $2.50.
"He has given us a life-picture. Europe is done in a style that must serve as an invaluable guide to those who go 'over the ocean,' as well as an interesting companion." — *Halifax Citizen.*

Sold by all booksellers, and sent by mail, postpaid, on receipt of price

LEE AND SHEPARD Publishers Boston

NARRATIVES OF NOTED TRAVELLERS

GERMANY SEEN WITHOUT SPECTACLES; or, Random Sketches of Various Subjects, Penned from Different Standpoints in the Empire
By HENRY RUGGLES, late United States Consul at the Island of Malta, and at Barcelona, Spain. $1.50.

"Mr. Ruggles writes briskly: he chats and gossips, slashing right and left with stout American prejudices, and has made withal a most entertaining book." — *New-York Tribune.*

TRAVELS AND OBSERVATIONS IN THE ORIENT, with a Hasty Flight in the Countries of Europe
By WALTER HARRIMAN (ex-Governor of New Hampshire). $1.50.

"The author, in his graphic description of these sacred localities, refers with great aptness to scenes and personages which history has made famous It is a chatty narrative of travel." — *Concord Monitor.*

FORE AND AFT
A Story of Actual Sea-Life. By ROBERT B. DIXON, M.D. $1.25.

Travels in Mexico, with vivid descriptions of manners and customs, form a large part of this striking narrative of a fourteen-months' voyage.

VOYAGE OF THE PAPER CANOE
A Geographical Journey of Twenty-five Hundred Miles from Quebec to the Gulf of Mexico. By NATHANIEL H. BISHOP. With numerous illustrations and maps specially prepared for this work. Crown 8vo. $1.50.

"Mr. Bishop did a very bold thing, and has described it with a happy mixture of spirit, keen observation, and *bonhomie.*" — *London Graphic.*

FOUR MONTHS IN A SNEAK-BOX
A Boat Voyage of Twenty-six Hundred Miles down the Ohio and Mississippi Rivers, and along the Gulf of Mexico. By NATHANIEL H. BISHOP. With numerous maps and illustrations. $1.50.

"His glowing pen-pictures of 'shanty-boat' life on the great rivers are true to life. His descriptions of persons and places are graphic." — *Zion's Herald.*

A THOUSAND MILES' WALK ACROSS SOUTH AMERICA, Over the Pampas and the Andes
By NATHANIEL H. BISHOP. Crown 8vo. New edition. Illustrated. $1.50.

"Mr. Bishop made this journey when a boy of sixteen, has never forgotten it, and tells it in such a way that the reader will always remember it, and wish there had been more."

CAMPS IN THE CARIBBEES
Being the Adventures of a Naturalist Bird-hunting in the West-India Islands. By FRED A. OBER. New edition. With maps and illustrations. $1.50.

"During two years he visited mountains, forests, and people, that few, if any, tourists had ever reached before. He carried his camera with him, and photographed from nature the scenes by which the book is illustrated." — *Louisville Courier-Journal.*

ENGLAND FROM A BACK WINDOW; With Views of Scotland and Ireland
By J. M. BAILEY, the "'Danbury News' Man." 12mo. $1.00.

"The peculiar humor of this writer is well known. The British Isles have never before been looked at in just the same way, — at least, not by any one who has notified us of the fact. Mr. Bailey's travels possess, accordingly, a value of their own for the reader, no matter how many previous records of journeys in the mother country he may have read." — *Rochester Express.*

Sold by all booksellers, and sent by mail, postpaid, on receipt of price

LEE AND SHEPARD Publishers Boston

YOUNG FOLKS' BOOKS OF TRAVEL

DRIFTING ROUND THE WORLD; A Boy's Adventures by Sea and Land

By CAPT. CHARLES W. HALL, author of "Adrift in the Ice-Fields," "The Great Bonanza," etc. With numerous full-page and letter-press illustrations. Royal 8vo. Handsome cover. $1.75. Cloth, gilt, $2.50.

"Out of the beaten track" in its course of travel, record of adventures, and descriptions of life in Greenland, Labrador, Ireland, Scotland, England, France, Holland, Russia, Asia, Siberia, and Alaska. Its hero is young, bold, and adventurous; and the book is in every way interesting and attractive.

EDWARD GREEY'S JAPANESE SERIES

YOUNG AMERICANS IN JAPAN; or, The Adventures of the Jewett Family and their Friend Oto Nambo

With 170 full-page and letter-press illustrations. Royal 8vo, 7 x 9¼ inches. Handsomely illuminated cover. $1.75. Cloth, black and gold, $2.50.

This story, though essentially a work of fiction, is filled with interesting and truthful descriptions of the curious ways of living of the good people of the land of the rising sun.

THE WONDERFUL CITY OF TOKIO; or, The Further Adventures of the Jewett Family and their Friend Oto Nambo

With 169 illustrations. Royal 8vo, 7 x 9¼ inches. With cover in gold and colors, designed by the author. $1.75. Cloth, black and gold, $2.50.

"A book full of delightful information. The author has the happy gift of permitting the reader to view things as he saw them. The illustrations are mostly drawn by a Japanese artist, and are very unique." — *Chicago Herald*.

THE BEAR WORSHIPPERS OF YEZO AND THE ISLAND OF KARAFUTO; being the further Adventures of the Jewett Family and their Friend Oto Nambo

180 illustrations. Boards, $1.75. Cloth, $2.50.

Graphic pen and pencil pictures of the remarkable bearded people who live in the north of Japan. The illustrations are by native Japanese artists, and give queer pictures of a queer people, who have been seldom visited.

HARRY W. FRENCH'S BOOKS

OUR BOYS IN INDIA

The wanderings of two young Americans in Hindustan, with their exciting adventures on the sacred rivers and wild mountains. With 145 illustrations. Royal 8vo, 7 x 9¼ inches. Bound in emblematic covers of Oriental design, $1.75. Cloth, black and gold, $2.50.

While it has all the exciting interest of a romance, it is remarkably vivid in its pictures of manners and customs in the land of the Hindu. The illustrations are many and excellent.

OUR BOYS IN CHINA

The adventures of two young Americans, wrecked in the China Sea on their return from India, with their strange wanderings through the Chinese Empire. 188 illustrations. Boards, ornamental covers in colors and gold, $1.75. Cloth, $2.50.

This gives the further adventures of "Our Boys" of India fame in the land of Teas and Queues.

Sold by all booksellers, and sent by mail, postpaid, on receipt of price

LEE AND SHEPARD Publishers Boston

IRENE E. JEROME'S • • • •
• • • • • • ART BOOKS

IN A FAIR COUNTRY. With 55 full-page illustrations; engraved by Andrew. Nearly 100 pages of text, by Thomas Wentworth Higginson. Gold cloth, full gilt, $6.00; Turkey morocco, $15.00; tree calf, $15.00; English seal style, $10.00.

Miss Jerome has caught the very glamour of the woodland and the lea with her pencil, transferring it to paper with the delicacy of an exquisite photograph, while Colonel Higginson's delightful style brings out the beauty of his topics most satisfactorily. As a specimen of the bookmaker's art, the volume leaves nothing to be asked.

A BUNCH OF VIOLETS. Original illustrations, engraved on wood and printed under the direction of GEORGE T. ANDREW. 4to, cloth, $3.75; Turkey morocco, $9.00; tree calf, $9.00; English seal style, $7.00.

The new volume is akin to the former triumphs of this favorite artist, whose "Sketch Books" have achieved a popularity unequalled in the history of fine art publications. In the profusion of designs, originality, and delicacy of treatment, the charming sketches of mountain, meadow, lake, and forest scenery of New England here reproduced are unexcelled. After the wealth of illustration which this student of nature has poured into the lap of art, to produce a volume in which there is no deterioration of power or beauty, but, if possible, increased strength and enlargement of ideas, gives assurance that the foremost female artist in America will hold the hearts of her legion of admirers.

NATURE'S HALLELUJAH. Presented in a series of nearly fifty full-page original illustrations (9½ x 14 inches), engraved on wood by GEORGE T. ANDREW. Elegantly bound in gold cloth, full gilt, gilt edges, $6.00; Turkey morocco, $15.00; tree calf, $15.00; English seal style, $10.00.

This volume has won the most cordial praise on both sides of the water. Mr. Francis H. Underwood, U. S. Consul at Glasgow, writes concerning it: "I have never seen anything superior, if equal, to the delicacy and finish of the engravings, and the perfection of the press-work. The copy you sent me has been looked over with evident and unfeigned delight by many people of artistic taste. Every one frankly says, 'It is impossible to produce such effects here,' and, whether it is possible or not, I am sure it is *not done;* no such effects are produced on this side of the Atlantic. In this combination of art and workmanship, the United States leads the world; and you have a right to be proud of the honor of presenting such a specimen to the public."

ONE YEAR'S SKETCH BOOK. Containing forty-six full-page original illustrations, engraved on wood by ANDREW; in same bindings and at same prices as "Nature's Hallelujah."

"Every thick, creamy page is embellished by some gems of art. Sometimes it is but a dash and a few trembling strokes; at others an impressive landscape, but in all and through all runs the master touch. Miss Jerome has the genius of an Angelo, and the execution of a Guido. The beauty of the sketches will be apparent to all, having been taken from our unrivalled New England scenery." — *Washington Chronicle.*

THE MESSAGE OF THE BLUEBIRD, Told to Me to Tell to Others. Original illustrations engraved on wood by ANDREW. Cloth and gold, $2.00; palatine boards, ribbon ornaments, $1.00.

"In its new bindings is one of the daintiest combinations of song and illustration ever published, exhibiting in a marked degree the fine poetic taste and wonderfully artistic touch which render this author's works so popular. The pictures are exquisite, and the verses exceedingly graceful, appealing to the highest sensibilities. The little volume ranks among the choicest of holiday souvenirs, and is beautiful and pleasing." — *Boston Transcript.*

Sold by all booksellers, and sent by mail, postpaid, on receipt of price
LEE AND SHEPARD Publishers Boston

www.ingramcontent.com/pod-product-compliance
Lightning Source LLC
Chambersburg PA
CBHW031811230426
43669CB00009B/1100